HOW TO STAY LOVERS WHILE RAISING YOUR CHILDREN

BY ANNE MAYER

PRICE STERN SLOAN
Los Angeles

© 1990 by Anne Mayer
Published by Price Stern Sloan, Inc.
360 N. La Cienega Boulevard
Los Angeles, California 90048
Printed in U.S.A.

9 8 7 6 5 4 3 2 1

Notice: All information in this book is given without guarantees on the part of the authors, contributors, consultants or publisher. Names and other biographical information about people mentioned in this book have been changed to protect the participants' privacy.

Mayer, Anne.
   How to stay lovers while raising your children : a burned-out parents' guide to sex / by Anne Mayer.
      p.   cm.
ISBN 0-89586-838-5
   1. Parents—United States—Time Management. 2. Parents—United States—Sexual behavior.   I. Title.
HQ755.8.M39   1990
646.7'8—dc20   89-24266
                                                           CIP

Recognizing the importance of preserving that which has been written, Price Stern Sloan, Inc. has decided to print this book on acid-free paper, and will continue to print the majority of the books it publishes on acid-free paper.

To David, my husband, lover and best friend, whose spontaneous love of life has helped me to believe that anything is possible; to Lindsay and Ashley, who have shown me a very special world through their eyes; to my parents Carol and Joe, for their encouragement; to Marolyn, my mother-in-law, for her loving wisdom; and to all parents everywhere who are ever striving to stay lovers while being nurturing mothers and fathers, too. . .

ACKNOWLEDGMENTS

My sincere thanks goes to Joani Blank, Marty Klein, Dr. Debora Phillips, Eileen Shiff, M.S., Dr. Douglas Sprenkle and Blake Rodgers for their extremely helpful insights. I am also grateful for the creative wisdom of others and am pleased to acknowledge them: Dr. Ruth K. Westheimer, Drs. William H. Masters and Virginia E. Johnson, Dr. Lonnie Barbach, Dr. Alan Loy McGinnis, Dr. Bernie Zilbergeld, Dr. Sanford J. Matthews, Dr. Paul Pearsall, Dr. Ayala M. Pines, Dr. Georgia Witkin-Lanoil, Dr. Avodah K. Offit, Dr. Marvin Silverman and Dr. David A. Lustig.

I am most happy to recognize the following individuals who helped to provide ways for me to reach many of the parents I interviewed for this book: Barbara Posner, Lynn Pooley, Robbie Wright, Glory Dierker, Ruth Viens, Mary Jane Smith, Ellie Rieth, John Accrocco, Dan Accrocco, Joy Blackiston, Sheila Hayes, Joyce Brown, Roberta Hoechster, Leslie Kane, Larry MacPhee, Lisa Vertelney, Nancy Wheeler, Leanne Slayton, Barbara Fuller, Harriet Stambaugh, Jan Altman and Donna Newton.

I would also like to extend a special thank you to Jim Sullivan and the other kind librarians at the Corte Madera Library; to my colleagues at the American Society of Journalists and Authors, Inc., who provided me with invaluable resources in researching the book; and to Terri Gelbaum, Sigrid Hoffman and Marie Sooper, who so often helped me out by watching my kids so I could work on this project.

And my most sincere appreciation goes to my agent Jeff Herman, who believed in me and encouraged me to make my dream a goal; to my editor Digby Diehl, who was responsive, supportive and a delight to work with; to my publisher, Nick Clemente, who believed in this project; to editor Gina Gross and to assistant editor Corrine Johnson, who helped carry this book to its completion.

TABLE OF CONTENTS

Introduction

When I became a mother for the first time, and returned to the doctor's office for my six-week check-up after the birth of my oldest daughter, my gynecologist blithely said I could ". . .resume sexual relations as usual."

When I left his office I felt angry. I loved my daughter dearly and my husband and I were thrilled to have her, but when we brought our baby home, it felt as though we had been hit by a tornado. Our lives had been turned upside down. Suddenly, all the usual ways we had of doing things—even the way we felt about ourselves as individuals and as a couple had to be altered or adjusted. To me, it seemed like someone had thrown a deck of cards, which represented our life together, into the air and as these cards came scattering to the ground, we had to scramble to put them into some new arrangement we could live with. *Sex* as usual? *Life* as usual? My doctor had to be joking!

Life does not continue "as usual" once our children are born. We all know this. If you don't know this and are expecting your first child, or merely contemplating parenthood at this point, read on and prepare yourselves. As parents, our lives, on a daily basis, range from crazy or semi-crazy, to nearly calm, on a rare day. We are either getting up three times a night to nurse our babies, changing enough diapers daily to fill a circus tent or driving our children to so many sports and social events that we can rightly be called "Chauffeur of the Year"! It confounds me, however, that parents are still given social messages that are not only false, but cause confusion, frustration and disappointment.

Society has led us to believe that our lives will go on as usual, so that we end up feeling disappointed and inadequate when our sexual lives (in fact, our lives in general) are not what they used to be. Society also tells us to accept the fact that life has changed. We should no longer concern ourselves with having a good sex life, or a quality life for that matter. Parenthood, itself, is supposed to be totally fulfilling 24 hours a day and if you are not satisfied, then something is *wrong* with *you!*

Even before our children are born, sex becomes a taboo subject. Childbirth classes talk about pregnancy, labor and childbirth, but do little, if anything, to help prepare couples for the tremendous emotional and physical upheaval they will experience in their sex lives.

Childbirth educator Sheila Kitzinger, further makes this point: ". . .somehow it is not quite nice to do it and you are both going to be rotten parents if you do. . . you must settle down to being a mom and dad with only maternal and paternal feelings of tender protectiveness towards the baby; sexual passion is considered to be a bit risky, even endangering the developing life. . ." [1] No where in this so-called conventional wisdom are a parent's individual needs considered. Certainly, no extensive, helpful sexual information for after the baby comes is offered. In fact, few people, if any, believe that parents are lovers, too. As a result, parents are left to fall into their own emotional and sexual traps—to feel alone, confused, frightened—often overwhelmed, depressed and in a phrase, *burned out.*

Raising happy, healthy children and trying to stay lovers *is* difficult. The second that "bundle of joy" we call a baby is born, there is an immediate and indefinite loss of time, energy and privacy for sex. But this does not mean you can't have a good sex life again. In fact, it is possible to have a "better" sex life.

While the basis of a truly happy sex life is a matter of expressing your real feelings to your spouse about what is bothering you, and what you want and need, it is also a matter of being a *smart sexual strategist*. As parents, when you think of sex, you are going to have to think of a strategy, too. For example, you may not be able to make love in your living room at high noon on a Saturday anymore, but you can lock your bedroom door and make love while the kids are downstairs watching cartoons at nine o'clock in the morning. Or, you may not be able to kiss each other passionately in the kitchen while making veal scaloppine anymore, but you can flirt and steal kisses, while preparing the lasagna.

Flirting with your spouse can help you feel less stressed out, and add a sense of sexual excitement to prepare you for sex later—after the children are in bed. It can help you to feel connected emotionally and physically, and boost your self-esteem. In fact, when you set a pattern of "flirting with your spouse" in motion, you help to establish a *loving sexual attitude*.

More than anything else, it is this loving sexual attitude, combined with an ability to express your feelings and to utilize sexual strategies, that can make the difference between a ho-hum sex life, and a "honey-I-can't-wait-to-be-with-you!" sex life. Parents have a right to *be* lovers and to *act* like lovers.

In my quest to find sexual strategies that help parents be the lovers they want to be, I sent out over 1,000 questionnaires to mothers and fathers. I gathered hundreds of stories, insights and opinions from parents who have been married for varied lengths of time, and who have children from the infant stage on up through the teen-age years. The purpose of my book is twofold. First, I wanted to discover the problems parents have encountered as lovers, and the solutions they have found that have brought them together and kept them close and express that. I also want to offer hope, encouragement and support to all parents with the message that *you are not alone* in your fears and concerns. As parents, we have *all* experienced our difficulties in trying to maintain a loving, sexual relationship with our spouses, while at the same time, striving to be loving mothers and fathers. Even if the love you feel for your spouse is not burning very brightly right now, there is help and hope for you as long as you are willing to work together for it.

Secondly, by seeking the insights of marriage and family counselors and sex therapists, I have discovered step-by-step guidelines on how to create and maintain a loving sexual life. I offer ways to:

- ♥ break free from the myths that can hurt your sexual self-esteem
- ♥ prioritize your life in order to get private time together
- ♥ deal with the daily difficulties of parenting that can affect your desire for sex
- ♥ handle interruptions, whether you are trying to have a conversation or make love
- ♥ find and develop your child-care support system so you can get away together; or take a mini "Intimacy Island" vacation when you cannot physically get away
- ♥ court each other again and be spontaneous when spontaneity, as you knew it, is gone
- ♥ take charge of your life so you can look and feel good for yourself and your spouse
- ♥ grab some "self time," so you will feel more relaxed
- ♥ accept and express your sexuality to develop a more sensual relationship
- ♥ strengthen your emotional bond, to survive better the stresses of life that can tear you apart

In addition, I have included basic tips to help you cope with the many invasions of privacy you have encountered or may encounter: when you are kissing in front of a cozy fire and your son comes downstairs to tell you he just wet the bed; when your daughter discovers Mommy's diaphragm case makes a great purse; when your children finally realize that all those noises coming from the master bedroom are not really King Kong and Godzilla on video.

In exploring the many ways to be lovers, you will begin to see the difficulties of parenthood not as roadblocks to a satisfying emotional and physical relationship, but as fences that can be hurdled together, along paths that can lead to a greater understanding and love for each other.

Trying to be good lovers while also trying to be patient, loving parents is a struggle, but there are many rewards to be gained. Most importantly, you will gain a sense of increased self-esteem as you begin to take charge of your life, and realize that when you take care of *your* needs, you are putting yourself in a much better position to deal with the demands of parenthood. And when you focus on your love for each other and do not put it constantly at the bottom of your priority list, you are creating a less tense, happier environment for everyone. Please let me know of your experiences. I invite you to share your insights, questions and opinions in order to help you help other mothers and fathers. You can write to me at: P.0. Box 788, Larkspur, California 94939-0788. I promise I will answer your letters. In the meantime, happy loving!

1
The Sex Hex

How We Lose Ourselves
When the Kids Are Born

Today, more than ever, couples want the "You-Can-Have-It-All" fantasy of a peaceful home environment, fulfilling careers, smart, happy kids and equal relationships. The problem is that we often are not getting our wishes fulfilled because we are not mere parents. We are "super parents," and have allowed our love for each other to exist only when we have time. The difficulty in contemporary American marriages, relate authors Carole Rafferty and Mark K. Powelson, is: "Time together, the precious binding glue of marriages, seems to be at an all-time low. Everything from careers to commuting time to the extraordinary explosion of leisure-time options (video, computers, self-improvement, adult education, television) means that the time left over for sustaining the relationship is shrinking, not expanding." [1] Perhaps the Disney movie, *Honey, I Shrunk the Kids,* was trying to tell us something. Or, perhaps it was merely tapping into every parent's occasional fantasy.

The super parent syndrome is the work ethic that carried to an extreme, takes an inevitable toll on sexual pleasure. Show me a sexually frustrated dad or mom ready to hop in the sack, and I'll show you an equally guilt-ridden spouse who feels obligated to take little Sally to soccer practice, swimming lessons and ballet class starting at dawn. When time together as a couple is at the bottom of the priority list, not only is the bond between you weakened, it can also make you feel like less of a sexual person.

During the course of interviewing numerous parents, I had a very enlightening conversation with one frustrated father about the definition of sex appeal. "Sex appeal?" he questioned. "Oh yes! That's when the husband appeals to his wife for sex!" I'm not saying we ignore our children and their needs. Children can bring great joy to a marriage and to our lives as a whole. They deserve our love and attention. But there is great harm in *over-committing* ourselves to our children and not spending the time necessary to maintain our marital relationships. Recent divorce statistics conclude that at least three-and-a-half million people, including children, are involved in a divorce each year. While there are many reasons for divorce—irreconcilable differences, spouse abuse, extramarital affairs—the one factor that has not been considered is this "sexless-servants-of-children" role we seem bent on boxing ourselves into. When we neglect our needs, not only do *we* suffer, but more importantly, our *children* suffer. They suffer from our resentments, our frustrations and our troubled relationships.

When my husband and I were new parents, we had no strategies for finding time to be lovers. We rarely went out together or allowed ourselves time just to relax. In fact, the idea of having a baby sitter take our daughter for a long walk in the park on a Sunday afternoon, so we could have some time together in our own home, never occurred to us.

I will never forget those early months when my oldest daughter was an infant. She would awaken at least three times in the night to nurse and only took a twenty-minute nap during the day, a schedule that continued for nine months. At my lowest point ever, I remember rocking my daughter in her rocking chair, trying to get her to go to sleep, so I could work on an overdue writing assignment. I was emotionally torn. I wanted to be a good mother. I wanted a successful career. I wanted a fabulous marriage. I wanted it all right then and there! When my husband came home from work that night, he was saddened to hear me say through eyes full of tears, "There is no joy in life anymore!"

Here I had a beautiful daughter, a part-time writing career, a lovely home and a husband who adored me. How could I feel such a thing? But my self-esteem had hit rock bottom. I didn't know who I was as a person anymore, or who we were as a couple or a family. By the time we got our daughter to sleep at night and our own heads hit the pillow, the last thing on our minds was sex, or even a stimulating

ROMANTIC WAYS TO DATE YOUR SPOUSE

♥ Ask your pediatrician, the director of your local parent support group, the director of your child's nursery school, your minister or rabbi, friends and neighbors for names of reliable baby sitters so that the two of you can spend some quality time together.

♥ Send your husband flowers to his office with a note attached, asking him out on a date. A friend of mine did this, and her husband was totally taken by surprise and thoroughly flattered: "No one ever sent me flowers before!" he exclaimed.

♥ Call your wife on the telephone and ask her for a date the way you used to. Or, you can do what Malcom, a father of an eight-year-old daughter and five-year-old son, did. He snuck out the back door one night and ran around to his front door. He rang the doorbell and when his wife Lynda answered the door, he gave her a single rose and asked her for a date. "I felt like a school girl again," she told me.

♥ Share a soda with two straws or a dessert with two forks, when out on a date. One father and mother who have two teen-age boys, tell me that sharing like this makes them feel like young romantics.

♥ Form a baby-sitting co-op with your neighbor. Ask her to watch your kids at her home for an evening, in exchange for taking her kids for an evening. Make sure the children are out of the house by the time your husband comes home from work. Prepare a nice dinner at home and don't let the last course be dessert.

♥ Go to sleep the same time your kids do one night, then set your alarm to go off one hour earlier and have a quiet breakfast date with your spouse before the children wake up.

conversation. We just wanted to go to sleep because we were *so exhausted*!

We decided something had to be done, or any semblance of a love life, or even a happy family life, would be lost. So we started dating

---

BUILDING A STRONG COUPLE FOUNDATION

♥ Schedule one hour a week, either in your home or on a date, to talk about what each of you is feeling. This is not a time to discuss what is happening with the kids, your job and the house, but rather just what is going on emotionally inside yourself.

♥ Schedule a "date night," which is one evening a week, where just the two of you go out to have fun.

♥ Take time to nurture yourself at least once a week. Have your husband watch the kids, while you have a cup of coffee and read the newspaper for an hour. Have your wife watch the children, while you go browse through a bookstore or take a nap.

♥ Surprise each other. Put a love note in your husband's wallet, your wife's purse or attach a love note to the front door so it is the first thing your spouse sees when he or she comes home from a hard day at work.

♥ Find a reliable overnight baby sitter, and spend more time than just an evening together. Very few couples do this. Why? Primarily because of feeling guilty about leaving their children. As Barbara, a mother of two sons ages three and seven, who recently went away with her husband for the first time in eight years, told me: "Once we did get away, we realized how sad it was not to have done this before. We just thought our kids would wither up if we weren't around all night. But they did fine. In fact, our oldest son keeps asking me when Mary is going to baby-sit overnight again. I was shocked!"

♥ Make eye contact with your spouse, and tell him or her "I love you!" at least once a week. Many times we may show our spouses how much we care by the special things we do, but it is so nice to hear how much we are loved!

---

each other again—and talking, and talking, and began to realize that we, as a couple, had to come first in order for a sense of harmony to be established in our lives. We knew that developing a new love life for ourselves would take lots of work but we were willing to work hard for it, not only for our own happiness, but for our children's happiness as well. We believed that if *we* were happy, our children would be happy, too.

In our own lives, and in the lives of the parents I have interviewed for this book, our "happy couple" theory has proven to be true. As life goes on, and the struggles and stresses of a life that includes children go on, creating and maintaining a loving, sexual life for yourselves *is* possible. Staying lovers with your spouse is, in fact, a key element to keeping harmony within the family as a unit. If you have a strong couple foundation, it is much more likely to happen that you will also have a strong family foundation.

STORIES OF CHANGE: STORIES OF HOPE

Let's look at some of the crises other parents have gone through, and examine the solutions that actually have made them closer and cemented their bond as lovers. Often, their struggles were not easy ones, but their determination to be close and to stay close paid off. Not only did they become couples again, but they became families again.

Jennifer and Tony

Both in their mid-thirties, Jennifer and Tony have one daughter, Jessie, now five years old. Jennifer left her career as a professional dancer to be home with Jessie, and Tony runs his own computer marketing business. They live in a suburb near San Francisco. Their active love life changed drastically when their daughter was born.

Jennifer

"We used to make love every single night without fail before Jessie was born. Once she came along, however, sex just got lost in the shuffle of parenthood, and five days would go by before we would realize that something was missing. Jessie was a very demanding baby and in the beginning she cried constantly, so we were too exhausted even to think about sex.

"At times when we did have sex, we never expected to be interrupted, but it does happen. When Jessie was two years old, Tony and I were making love in our bedroom after she had gone to sleep. It was dark. We were getting very passionate with each other. Suddenly, I felt these little baby hands on my shoulder, and realized that Jessie had climbed out of her crib. When I whispered in Tony's ear, 'The *baby*! The *baby*!' he thought I was saying, 'Oh, *baby*! Oh, *baby*!' When he finally understood what I was really saying, that 'It's *the baby*!' he flew to the other side of the room in one second. It always amazed me how he did that! Thank goodness it was so black in the room. She couldn't really see us. . . it might have frightened her. We tried to deal calmly with the periodic interruptions, which were frustrating. When she was three years old, we finally got a break because she went to preschool three mornings a week. I remember our first morning away from her. Tony and I went to register my car, then we went back home and made love. It was great! For the first time since we became parents, we could have some private time together. We could make love without worrying about her crying and interrupting us and we just loved it! We just loved preschool!"

Tony

"Since I own my own business, I am able to be fairly flexible with my schedule. If we are too tired at night to make love, or are interrupted, Jennifer and I will spend time in the morning together, either before Jessie wakes up or after she goes to school. Sometimes I'll come home for lunch and see Jennifer. When you have kids, you have to learn to be flexible."

As Jennifer and Tony realized, having a child or children in the home forces parents to reevaluate how they spend their time together as a couple. This does not mean you give up trying to find ways to make love. It means that sometimes you have to rearrange schedules, hire a baby sitter or simply lock your bedroom door. You must work harder to get some time together. Planning your time for making love or just for talking does not take away from romance. It creates the opportunity for it.

Pam and John

A couple in their late thirties, both Pam and John work full time, plus care for their three active boys, ages ten, eight and five. Pam is a teacher in special education, and John is an insurance salesman. They live in the suburbs, just outside Columbus, Ohio. Pam describes their home life as a three-ring circus, but still they have managed to find time to be lovers.

Pam

"We went from making love passionately every night, to not making love for a year after our first son was born. Making love every night was what I really thought marriage was all about. In the beginning, John and I felt a real embarrassment about our non-sex life, and it wasn't until we shared our feelings with close friends that we realized we weren't the only ones. Now, three children later, our sex life is good, but we don't make love every night.

"After the birth of each one of my children I felt fat and not very comfortable with my body. I never felt sexy or desired sex as much when I felt fat. I watched my diet and exercised, and subsequently, lost the extra weight so I could fit into my sexy teddy. At one point in our marriage when I thought I was losing John in our sex life, I started wearing my teddy to do laundry in the laundry room, which is next door to his den where he works on his computer. I would waltz in there in the evenings after our kids were in bed and ask John if he wanted a snack or any laundry done. At that point, he would always come upstairs with me.

"Even when there was this ebb and flow in our sexual life, we have always managed to stay in touch. We call each other on the telephone and sing love songs to each other. Other times, I will put positive reinforcement cards in his wallet that say something like: 'You can do it! Have a nice day! I'm horny for you!'

"I guess one big way we stay in touch is knowing that we are really there for each other. I know if anything needs to be discussed and I say to John, 'I need to talk to you,' he will stop what he is doing and will talk to me. This to me is the biggest comfort, the best thing I can have in a relationship. Or, when we make love, and he gives me that special tender look. I'm not saying I get that look every time we make love, but when I do, it's like the first time. . . We also have a date every Saturday night, in order to stay in touch. I don't care how wonderful you think your relationship is, or how much you feel you can trust your spouse, you are always vulnerable. You must always work on your relationship. If you have found somebody you really get along well with, it is a gift and you have to nurture it."

John

"It seemed after our first child was born, that was the end of my chance to come home after working all day and relax. Everything in terms of having any self time or couple time had shifted, and it took a while to work things out. For a while I was angry. I yelled at Pam a lot, and yelled at our son. We both argued a lot in front of him. When our second child was born, and then when the third one came along, we went from having our evenings to ourselves, to having no time together until ten o'clock at night. So, we often are too tired for sex. But one thing that has helped is Pam will fix dinner, and give me a chance to read the newspaper and rest. Then later, I will put our children to bed and while I'm doing that, Pam will take a nap. At least we will feel a little more energized when we want to make love. We have also started making love downstairs on our living room couch, so our kids won't hear us and we can have more privacy. Another way we stay in touch is Pam and I will frequently have lunch together when the children are in school."

Staying in touch by surprising each other with thoughtful gestures, and being considerate of one another's needs, goes a long way toward creating the desire for sex. If you are struggling to make some sense out of your hectic evening schedule of fixing dinner and getting the children to bed, talk about how you can give each other just a half-hour break, so that when things finally quiet down, you will have energy for sex.

Kara and Charles

In their early forties, Kara and Charles have two children, a boy, age nine, and a girl, four. Kara works part time as an interior designer, and Charles is an executive for a large advertising firm. They live in a small suburb, an hour outside New York City. Charles commutes to work on the train everyday. When Kara was pregnant with their son, they began experiencing problems not only in their sex life, but in their marriage and in their individual lives. Fortunately, they were wise enough to seek the help they needed.

Kara

"Shortly after Charles and I married, my father passed away, and I started getting these terrible anxiety attacks. I thought I was dying. I became more clingy to Charles, more dependent on him. I tried to talk to Charles about my anxieties, but he thought they were silly and that it was ridiculous that I was having them.

"When our son was born, I cherished him because I wanted to have a child so much. I desperately wanted to give him the love and attention I never got. My mother was an alcoholic and my father was a drug addict, and they were incapable of caring for my two older brothers and me. We were shipped off to boarding schools and camps, so I never really knew my parents. The two people I became very close to when I was very young, my nanny and her husband, were fired because my parents didn't like the fact that I only wanted to be with these people. I even started thinking of them as my parents. For a while after they were fired, my brothers and I were getting our own breakfast, walking a mile to the train station to catch the train to go to school, then riding a bus home, all by ourselves. I was six years old at the time. My anxiety attacks, I later learned through therapy, were caused by my great fear of being abandoned.

"During the time I was pregnant and after our son was born, my husband had been having an affair. I found out about it when our son was nine months old. I was shocked. Even though our son was young, I'm sure he was affected by all the anger and tears. My husband and I decided we should seek marital counseling. After talking during two sessions with our therapist, we decided to do what is called a planned separation. We separated for three months and set a date when we would come together and decide if we would get a divorce or get back together. We decided to get back together. During this time we each started seeing our therapist separately. We realized we had deep-seated emotional pain from both our childhoods that we had to work through, in order to resolve conflicts in our relationship.

"The affair happened ten years ago, but we still talk about it sometimes. Today, we are very happy together and have a good sex life. Being able to talk about past emotional childhood pain has helped us tremendously. It opened up a whole new relationship for us. The biggest relief was just the realization that it is all right to talk about your feelings. We are very open in expressing our feelings to each other, and we are very open with our kids. We both know how much it hurt us and our relationship not being able to express our true feelings, so we never squelch the expression of feelings or the need for affection in our household."

Charles

"The troubles that led up to my affair were a combination of things, not one specific thing. During the time Kara was pregnant and after our child was born, I was feeling very neglected. When Kara was pregnant, she was the one getting all the attention, and I was just the husband. When our child was born, I felt I had to compete for Kara's attention. She was not very interested in sex or even being with me. I wanted to be the primary person in Kara's life but felt I wasn't. At the same time, Kara seemed to be making so many demands on me. I felt that I had become just someone to do things for her. I had ceased to be Charles in her eyes. Instead, I was just a husband, a role.

"At work, however, I was a rising star. I was just made vice-president of my firm and I was aware of several ladies who were attracted to me. I became close to one particular lady, whom I just flirted with for several weeks. When we went out on a date three months later, I wasn't thinking about the consequences. I was just focused on what was happening, and here was someone who was giving me attention. The thing that would have been useful was seeking help *before* the affair happened, but problems don't usually happen all of a sudden. They sneak up on you. The advantage of this, is that if you are lucky, you have plenty of time to seek help. The disadvantage is that you don't notice you need help because problems crop up gradually. I never thought about seeing a marriage counselor back then, because I had this idea that if you were an insightful person you could work out your own problems; but this is not always the case.

"I had painful feelings from my own childhood experiences that played another factor in our marriage. My father was absent all the time, rarely talked to me and never showed me any affection. And my mother would deny I had any sad or angry feelings whenever I wanted to talk to her about them. After a while, I got so frustrated and angry, that I didn't talk to her about my feelings. I didn't talk to anyone about my feelings. I didn't deny them. I just didn't let anyone know what I was feeling inside.

"So, here I had come into our marriage with twenty years of not expressing my feelings. I didn't know how to talk to Kara about my feelings of neglect. Fortunately, a very good therapist was able to help me, and ultimately helped our marriage. One important lesson I learned in all of this is that if there is something you want to hide, you end up shutting off all important communication. If there is something you don't want to talk about, you end up talking about nothing. This not only affects the emotional aspects of your marriage, but the physical aspects, too. When we were experiencing all these difficult problems, there was very little affection and no sexual contact.

"Now, at least once a week, we set aside one hour to talk about what we are really feeling, which helps us to connect emotionally, and in turn creates a desire to connect sexually, too."

So often, when we grow up and go off on our own into the world like Kara and Charles, we tend to believe that any painful experiences, with our parents or with other people in our childhood, are in the past. We kid ourselves into believing that if we keep these feelings repressed, they won't bother us anymore. In reality, however, these painful feelings surface in our relationships with our spouse and our children to wreak havoc in our lives. If you are secretly carrying a burden of pain, talk to your spouse about it, even if you are afraid. Chances are, your spouse may have experienced some painful events in his or her lifetime, too. But together you can help each other. If you are having trouble working out these feelings by yourselves, then seek the professional guidance you need.

When you take care of yourselves and your relationship first, you are much better able to care for your children—to give them the love, guidance and attention they need. Couples I have spoken to confirm this belief. Being good to yourself is not selfish. Spending time with your spouse is not selfish. Deep down, children want their parents to be happy. When their parents are happy, they are happy, too. So be good to yourself, and in doing so, remember, you're being good role models for your children. You don't have to be a "super parent," to be super. Concentrate on building harmony within your relationship; and a harmony within your family is more likely to follow.

Points to Remember

1. You don't have to be everything to everybody all the time. Concentrate on building a loving, happy relationship with your spouse, first. If you are happy, your children will be happy. If you have a strong *couple foundation*, chances are you will more likely have a strong *family foundation*.

2. Take time to date your spouse. Set aside one night a week where you just have fun together.

3. Make time to talk about your feelings. Set aside one hour a week where you just discuss what is going on emotionally, inside yourself, with your spouse. Don't talk about the kids, the jobs, the house, the dog—just what you are feeling.

4. Don't neglect your own needs and allow frustration and resentment to build up. By taking care of yourself, you are taking care of your spouse and children too, who do not deserve to be the targets of your anger.

2
Sexpectations

How the Myths about Sex Appeal and Romance Keep Us from Having Both

Whether we are discussing romantic living, or life itself, it is our expectations that seem to trip us up more than anything else. In fact, our belief in the myths that dictate how life should be alters our expectations in almost everything we do, often with disappointing results. When our romantic fantasies do not pan out, like they always seem to do in the movies, we are left feeling that something must be wrong with us. Or that romance is better left to people without kids. Nonsense! Just because you are a parent doesn't mean you can no longer be sexy, or have romance in your life. But in order to be a romantic, sexy person and create romance, you have to separate the myths from the realities.

The cultural traps or myths that interfere with our ability to feel sexy and have romance abound. If you believe in them you will overlook the unique sexiness you do possess and miss opportunities to have romance. In talking with parents around the country, I have been able to isolate five myths that affect us the most, and keep us from being lovers.

MYTH: You must have a perfect body to have great sex.

REALITY: Love, understanding and communication are what makes sex great.

Many mothers who answered my questionnaire seemed particularly susceptible to this one. "Since having my two children, I've let myself get overweight, so I don't feel as alluring. It definitely affects my desire for sex," said a mother whose two sons are three-and-a-half and eight.

Husbands, however, were not as concerned with their wives' weight, as this father of a daughter and son related: "My wife gained weight while pregnant with our second child. She still feels fat, and unattractive. It doesn't bother me, but she won't believe that. This really saddens me because she must think that all I care about is how she looks."

If you don't feel good about the way you look, then it is important to do something about it, but don't set your sights so high that any measure of success with diet and weight loss will be a disappointment to you. The husbands I interviewed wanted their wives to feel good about themselves, but didn't feel their wives should have to look like some pencil thin model. When I asked husbands, "What is it about your spouse that excites you the most?" they were not concerned with just looks.

"My wife is very comfortable with her body, the way she carries herself," said a father of a one-year-old daughter. "She has a softness about her, something from within."

Men are also turned on by honesty, as this father of twin girls related about his wife: "She is very open about what she likes sexually, which is oral sex. I don't have to play twenty questions or try to read her mind. She lets me *know* that *this* turns her on! And I get excited knowing that this pleases her."

Familiarity and experience stimulated a sense of sex appeal. "She knows a lot more now about what I like best in lovemaking, and she is very attentive," a father of teen-agers, married twenty-two years, told me. "We have a perfect fit. We know each other so well," said the young dad of a baby boy.

One father of four children couldn't say enough about his wife. "She's a wonderful woman, perfect friend, great mom, excellent cook. She's just the best person I know."

Another dad with two children under four, felt it was exciting just being with his wife and loving her. "Now I have the extra benefit of being able to share her with our children."

Some husbands also said they were excited by their wives' ability to just have fun, to be a bit daring and "not wear any underwear beneath her dress," chimed the father of a two-and-a-half-year-old son. They were also greatly turned on by their wives' longing for them and by their ability to "take pleasure in sex." "My wife's intense desire for me is extremely exciting," related a middle-aged father.

> *"Although certain physical traits may attract initially, in the long run the ability to keep a mate interested is a matter of soul."* [1]
> —Dr. Alan Loy McGinnis, marriage and family therapist, minister and author of *The Romance Factor*

When I asked the wives what excited them the most about their husbands, the majority felt that, while they appreciated their spouses' efforts to stay in shape, they were turned on more by their ability to express feelings and be physically affectionate.

"My husband hugs me a lot and is open about his feelings. This definitely makes me desire him more sexually," said a mother of a four-year-old son.

"He can be very tender. He's a wonderful hugger and holder. I love his tenderness; he's very special in that way," related a mother of three children under six.

"I love his body and the way he moves and his small gestures that evoke real tenderness," a young mother of a baby girl told me.

Wives were particularly excited when their husbands not only expressed feelings, but allowed their wives to see the most vulnerable, intimate parts of themselves. This is the essence of an intimate relationship, when both spouses can open themselves completely to each other without fear of being ridiculed or rejected. One wife and mother of two teen-agers, who was turned on by her husband's ability to be vulnerable with her, loved him all the more because he accepted *her* vulnerabilities, too. "He loves me flaws and all."

Wives were also very excited by their husbands giving them compliments. Even if the wives didn't have perfect bodies, the husbands who complimented the features they did find attractive scored high marks. "My husband is very complimentary. This really helps in my feeling sexy and in desiring him," related a mother of a three-year-old son. "He'll say, 'Oh, that dress looks great on you,' or 'that color is really nice,' or 'you always look good when you wear that blouse,' or 'your skin feels so soft.' He's always saying something positive about my appearance."

HOW TO BOOST YOUR SPOUSE'S SEXUAL SELF-ESTEEM:
Husbands Compliment Your Wives!

♥ Hone in on something specific that she has done very well as a mother lately, and praise her, praise her, praise her! When a woman becomes a mother, her self-esteem becomes tied very closely to her job as a parent. And as parents, we are more often criticized, rather than complimented for the incredible job we do. If a woman does not feel very good about herself as a mother, she's not going to feel very good about herself in bed.

♥ Tell her that she excites you, and that you can't wait to make love with her. Your wife needs to hear that she is desirable, that you really "care" about spending time with her as a "person."

♥ "Listen" to her when she talks to you, and don't allow yourself to be distracted by the newspaper or the television. Put your paper down and turn off the TV!

Wives Compliment Your Husbands!

♥ Don't blast your husband with a daily report of which kid hit whom, and which kid got fingernail polish on the toilet, when he calls you from the office. Save it for later. Instead, thank him for calling, and tell him how wonderful it is to hear his voice.

♥ Tell him how great he looks just before you both go off for work in the morning.

♥ Create a calming, sexy environment for him to come home to. Yes, it's possible! Turn off the television. Turn on some mood music. Give the kids a snack. Then pour your husband a glass of wine, and put out some nice cheese and crackers. Dinner can wait half an hour. Let him know you are glad he's home.

Men also enhanced their wives' desire for them by showing consideration for their likes and dislikes regarding sex. "He just knows how to push all the right buttons," a mother of a ten-year-old son told me.

"His concern for my pleasure draws me closer to him," recalled the mother of three children; eight, six and three. "I like his inventiveness and attentiveness."

Family commitment was a turn-on for many wives. "When I see my husband showing interest, tenderness and affection toward our sons, that excites me and makes me want to make love to him," a mother of a four-year-old and two-year-old told me. "He's loving and patient, a great daddy."

While husbands and wives do appreciate their spouses' efforts to stay physically healthy, talking, touching, laughing and showing undivided attention and consideration are the elements that arouse passion. You don't have to be Mr. Atlas or Miss Universe to create your own sexual highs.

MYTH: If you aren't having sexual intercourse all the time, something is wrong with you.

REALITY: Everyone's sex life slows down after children are born.

Of the parents who filled out my questionnaire, the majority said that they had sexual intercourse an average of four times a month or less, and had sexual intercourse mostly on the weekends. As a result of the heavy demands of children, plus juggling careers and duties at home, parents today are engaging in weekend sex.

Does this make us all oddballs? Certainly not. While many of the parents stated that they would like to have sex more often, you are not going to lose it, if you wait until the weekend to use it. By pressuring yourselves to have sex more frequently than you are able, you may pressure yourselves into not desiring sex.

"Since we do not need to have sex to survive, most physical and emotional dangers will diminish sexual desire. We usually allow sexual desire to emerge under safe circumstances and inhibit it in situations we believe to be unsafe." [2]
—Lonnie Barbach, psychologist and sex therapist

A person's sex drive, his or her innate physiological desire for sex, is entirely an individual matter and will vary at any particular time depending on environmental, emotional and physical factors. As parents, we certainly have our fill of these factors. To be more specific, factors most likely to affect parents' sex lives in general after children come along are: lack of time; lack of privacy; fatigue; resentments; financial burdens; children sleeping in their parents' beds; housework (not getting enough help); and low self-esteem. Fear of pregnancy was still a concern among a small minority of mothers.

In parenting children, factors most likely to affect sexual desire are: disagreements over disciplining the children; sibling rivalry; childrens' illnesses, such as colds, flu, coughs; concerns about how well the child is doing in school; worries over the child's sleeping habits; and worries over the child's separation anxieties.

All of these variables are enough to turn you into a celibate creature if you let them get to you and your love life. On one hand, pressuring yourselves to have sex might backfire on you. On the other hand, allowing these factors to dampen your sexual desire is not going to help either.

If you want to have sex more often, but something is killing your desire, ask yourself what it is. Are you angry because your spouse won't help you enough with the housework? Are you resentful because your child won't go to sleep unless he or she sleeps in your bed? Are you exhausted from playing referee all the time, when your kids fight with each other? Pinpoint exactly what it is that is causing you to feel the most stress and try to resolve it. If there are several issues wearing you down, don't try to solve them all at once. Pick the one issue that is giving you the most trouble, and work on that one first. Then take each problem at a time and deal with it.

When stresses get you down, don't blame each other; blame the situation. Get on the same team, and try to solve problems together. Blaming and insulting each other only makes matters worse.

Finally, remember that sex is not just sexual intercourse. And simply changing your pace of life a bit can enhance sexual desire. One mother told me that some of the hottest sex she ever experienced was on the dance floor, while she and her husband were doing some "dirty dancing." Another smart mom led her husband into the garage and into their van, after the kids went to bed. They got into some heavy necking and petting, just like they used to before the children were born. And a particularly intuitive dad brought home a massage book one night, and he and his wife gave each other a sensual massage.

MYTH: A knowledge of super sexual techniques is what makes sex great.

REALITY: Tenderness and attentiveness are more important than techniques.

Being lovers does not mean you have to be sexual acrobats. Your life on a daily basis is enough of a circus. A great sexual performance does not ensure that sexual intercourse will always be satisfying.

The opportunity for good sex begins when you tune into each other sexually, and take the time to talk to one another about your likes and dislikes regarding sex. If I sound like I'm pushing "communication" as the biggest sexual turn-on, you are right! This is because I spoke to many many couples who had either experienced a major conflict that almost split them up, or who were in the midst of marital counseling. They all told me that once they began opening up to one another and expressed their hurts and resentments and needs, without blame, they discovered a renewed intimacy, which in turn revived and strengthened their sexual desire for each other and their ability to experience great sex.

"Sometimes it makes you feel bad about saying things for fear of hurting the other person's ego, but my husband and I realized that the sooner we could be real candid with each other, the sooner we could get on with the way we wanted to live," said Judy, a mother of a toddler, who had allowed resentments to build up, which reduced her sexual pleasure with her husband. "I don't know how anyone can be fully satisfied with the physical connection, without first making the emotional connection. I just cannot enjoy sex if I am angry."

Other parents felt the same way. In my questionnaire, and during interviews with parents, I asked the question: What is the most enjoyable aspect of your sex life? I received fascinating answers:

"We are a lot more understanding and patient in our efforts to please one another. We know each other's needs," related Kathy, a mother of four children, ranging in age from eight to twenty-one. Her husband Bob, replied: "There is a lot of give and take in paying close attention to the other person's feelings. This existed before kids, but our years together have taught us a lot."

Carmen, the mother of a three-and-a-half-year-old told me: "I really enjoy sex with my husband. I don't always have an orgasm, but I can be satisfied with the touching and closeness."

ENHANCE YOUR LOVEMAKING THROUGH SEXUAL CONSIDERATION

♥ Try something new. Play out your sexual fantasies or introduce sex toys if this is something you have been wanting to do, but discuss these ideas together. If your spouse is not so keen on sex toys, for example, don't force the issue. Find something that appeals to both of you.

♥ Suggest something new, by saying: "I'm really in the mood for some hot stuff with you. I've been thinking about you all week; now it's the weekend and I want to give our lovemaking an extra oomph. What do you say I go get a film at the video store?" You *do not* say: "Honey, our sex life has been pretty lousy lately. Maybe this film will rev you up!"

♥ Take a shower. Brush your teeth. Husbands shave your beards. Wives shave your legs. Don't let a little thing like bad breath or hairy legs turn you off to each other and spoil your sex date.

♥ Share in the responsibility of preparing your sexual place. Husbands, if your wife is in the bathroom putting in her diaphragm, then you get out the towels and light the candle. Wives, if your husband is still in the bathroom shaving, then you turn on the romantic music, or put the film in your VCR.

♥ Tune into the verbal and manual signals your spouse sends you during lovemaking, about what specific stimulation he or she likes. Higher does not mean lower, and lower does not mean higher. Sharing, caring, giving were the three words parents used when describing the most enjoyable aspects of their sex lives, which sums up technique. To be more precise, technique has to do with our ability to talk, listen and understand. If you would like more caressing and kissing, more help in reaching orgasm, more oral sex, more variety if sex has become too routine, talk to your spouse about it.

Terri, the mother of a son, three, and daughter, six, seemed grateful to her husband for taking the time to listen. "I can finally have orgasms thanks to him."

"Our pleasure with each other's bodies continues to increase with experience and knowing each other," related Diane, mother of a nine-year-old daughter. "Specifically, the most enjoyable aspect of our sex life is the sharing and closeness."

Although the difficulties of rearing children can take its toll on a parent's sex life, one father of two sons, four and eight, felt his sex life was enhanced by having kids. "After experiencing childbirth together, any inhibitions my wife and I may have had with each other were eliminated."

MYTH: Romance is for people without kids.

REALITY: Romance is for everyone.

A phrase one hears constantly when one becomes a parent is: "Well, he has finally 'settled down.' " Or, for couples contemplating parenthood, they are haunted with the question: "When are you two going to 'settle down' and raise a family?" What does this *mean*? Are we suppose to roll over and play dead and not laugh or have fun anymore? Are we suppose to turn into Ma and Pa Kettle and sit on the porch all day? Would our culture have us give up romantic living, the very element that not only can add spark and zest to our lives as a couple, but to our children's lives? What a ridiculous notion!

One of the greatest enemies of love these days is boredom. "For many couples who consider divorce, the problem is not that they have grown to hate each other. They are simply bored with each other," says Dr. McGinnis.[3] Boredom is obviously not beneficial for parents or their children. Romance, however, can greatly enhance love between spouses and siblings, and benefit the family as a whole.

Romance is a way of looking at life as a celebration, not as something we just survive. *And in order to have romance, this means you cannot let your life run you. You have to run your life!* The stresses of life are not going to go away, but you can manage them and celebrate life in spite of them. Having romance does not have to involve a lot of effort, time or money. It just takes a little imagination.

One night, my husband and I were getting romantic in bed and we heard a scream come from my younger daughter's bedroom. She had developed an acute ear infection, but did not tell us about it until her symptoms had gotten worse. She was crying hysterically, and we decided that my husband should take her to the emergency room at the hospital. They were there for three hours and finally returned home at three o'clock in the morning. My daughter was on antibiotics and finally sleeping soundly.

Neither my husband nor I got any sleep or lovemaking in that night, but I did something that added a lot of spark and helped us deal with the disappointment we felt at not having had our time alone together. I sent a cheese and fruit basket to him at his office with a mylar balloon and a note attached that read: "When the Going Gets Tough, the Tough Get Loving!"

CREATIVE WAYS TO EVOKE ROMANCE

- ♥ Put a single flower and a love note on your spouse's pillow.
- ♥ Buy some perfume your husband loves that you used to wear. Put some on, then give him a big hug.
- ♥ Find the sexiest card you can, spray some of this same perfume on it, and mail it to your husband at the office.
- ♥ Buy your wife some sexy black underwear, instead of flowers.
- ♥ Wash each other's hair.

MYTH: If you are not out dining and dancing you are not having romance.

REALITY: Romance is in the heart, not in the pocketbook.

If you believe you have to go out to have romance, you will never have romance. We all know it's not always easy to find baby sitters. If your kids *are* the baby sitters, it is not always easy to go out if you have to pick them up at the various social functions, such as football games or dances.

Many parents who answered my questionnaire and those whom I have interviewed, have discovered ways to be romantic and create romance without fully realizing it. They have just re-defined romance to suit their own needs on their own terms. Naturally, it would be nice to go out, and you should if you get the opportunity, but if you can't, this doesn't mean a romantic occasion has to be a fantasy.

> *"Having a magical relationship won't happen just because you are in love. You have to work to make the magic keep happening."* [4]
> —Barbara De Angelis, Ph.D., family therapist

Taking showers and baths together by candlelight seems to be big on the romantic hit list. Parents find this helps them relax and gives them a place to escape to. So, instead of rushing to the television set after the kids have gone to bed, or if they are older and are still up, lock your bathroom door and hop into the shower.

Back or foot massages are also popular. "We give each other ten-minute massages," revealed one smart mother of a toddler. "This helps relieve everyday stress and gets us in the mood for sex."

Another mother of teen-agers, married twenty-seven years, felt the same way. "Sometimes when I'm so tired I can't remember my name, and my muscles are hurting, my husband gives me a backrub or footrub, and it is a total turnaround, so that I do have energy for him physically."

Dressing up for each other as if you were going out, can add zest. Close friends of mine dress up for each other and take turns preparing special meals after their daughter goes to bed. If you want to dance, turn on your stereo and dance in the living room. Don't worry about feeling silly. Capture romance!

"Just find anything you can do together and there's romance in that," a mother of four teen-agers told me. "You can work in the kitchen together creating a nice meal, or work in the yard planting a beautiful garden of flowers. We sometimes tend to overlook our home as a resort. Often, we are being run by our house, instead of the other way around."

Part of the reason for this is that, as parents, we tend to always be racing in different directions as we try to get various jobs completed before we are interrupted by our children. The trick to finding romance, even when we are busy, is a matter of talking. We forget to ask for each other's help, which will bring us together. "I've started asking my wife if she would like to help me work in the yard, and just the idea that I've asked her shows respect for her feelings and this has greatly enhanced our intimacy," said a father of three young children. "This is so simple to do, so easy to lose."

"We've often had our most romantic conversations in the kitchen," one mother of a twelve-year-old daughter told me. Another mother of a three-year-old son and six-year-old daughter revealed: "For my husband and me, our feeling is that sex starts in the kitchen with sharing our day."

Romantic gestures mean a lot, and spouses who regularly surprised each other with acts of kindness greatly expanded their capacity for intimacy. Taking turns bringing each other coffee in the morning, letting each other sleep late on a Saturday morning, running a warm bath, leaving love notes under a pillow or holding hands in the movies can all help create a romantic environment and set the mood for sex.

"When my husband brings me a small gift and says: 'This looked like you,' or 'I thought of you when I saw this,' the feeling of being appreciated for who you are is very romantic," reflected the mom of ten-year-old twin boys.

When you are apart during the day, calls on the telephone can help you keep up the emotional connection. One couple makes a point to call each other frequently just to say how much they care.

When you do go out, don't just go to a restaurant. Try to do something different. Take a picnic to the beach or go to a nearby park. One friend of mine and her husband, whose children are ten and twenty-one, bought a boat and regularly drift slowly and romantically on the Hudson River. "The girls like to go on the boat with us, but they like to go fast," related Vicky. "Whenever my husband and I want to be alone, we tell them we are going to go slow, and they beg off."

Still another couple drives their van to a secluded spot and has dinner *à la* Chinese take-out. They are alone and away from the house.

If you have trouble thinking of romantic things to do with each other, remember the special moments you spent together during your courting days. Did you listen to music? Visit art galleries? Go bowling? Take long walks in the woods? Recently, my husband and I hired a baby sitter so we could take a long stroll at sunset by the bay near our home. Another time we went ice skating, just for fun. The idea is that it is all right to be a kid, too, sometimes—to laugh and joke and love life. Our children will thank us for it, because what greater sense of security can we give them, than our own happiness, our love for each other?

Points to Remember

1. Communication, consideration and understanding are the three main ingredients for good sex, not a perfect body.

2. Most parents have sex an average of four times a month. A person's sex drive is entirely an individual matter and will vary at any particular time, so there is nothing wrong with you if you don't have sex every night. Neither do you have to be sexual acrobats to have great sex. A good sex life depends on being attentive to one other's needs.

3. Romance is for everyone. You don't have to give up being romantic and having fun together now that you are parents. You have a right to be lovers and create romantic opportunities, however and whenever you can manage it.

3

Tunnel of Love or Tunnel Vision?

Getting Your Priorities Straight

There is a story about a man and his wife who are cleaning up the kitchen together one evening. The wife is washing dishes and has her back turned. Suddenly, the husband asks, "Do you want to go out?" "Oh yes!" answers the wife, who immediately drops what she is doing and dashes to grab her coat. The couple go out for coffee. The next day, the husband is talking to a colleague at the office about his evening, and sheepishly admits that it wasn't his wife he had asked to go out. It was the family dog who was lying on the kitchen floor!

This story is supposed to be a joke, of course, but actually, I would call it a tragedy. The couple had allowed their marriage to sink so low on their list of priorities that going for a walk with "Fido" had taken a higher place of importance over quality time the couple could spend together. They had begun to take each other for granted so often, that the wife was shocked when she heard her husband ask: "Do you want to go out?" This may be just a tale, but it is not far from the truth in many homes. The promise couples make to be number one in each other's hearts and minds at the time of marriage, soon becomes forgotten as other interests take on a higher priority.

"Any part of the marriage that is ignored will disappear and and this rule is particularly true for sex." [1]
    —Dr. Paul Pearsall, psychologist and director of
      the Problems of Daily Living Clinic,
      at Sinai Hospital, Detroit, Michigan

In a recent poll conducted by United Media Enterprises, for example, Americans picked watching television, fixing a leaky faucet and listening to music over making love with their mates.

With increased participation in interests and activities, it is no wonder couples complain about having no time for sex. If couples are parents, the lament is even louder because children, understandably so, take up a large portion of their parents' time. However, the

---

HOW AMERICANS SPEND THEIR TIME

ACTIVITY	PARTICIPATE EVERY DAY OR ALMOST EVERY DAY
Watching television	72%
Reading a newspaper	70%
Listening to music	46%
Exercising or jogging	35%
Talking with friends	30%
Reading a book	24%
Working in the garden	22%
Fixing or building things around the house	17%
Engaging in sex	11%

© 1983 Newspaper Enterprise Association, Inc. Reprinted by permission of NEA, Inc.

---

tendency is to allow children to take first place over the commitment to be lovers. Children often become the number one priority. Career advancement needs come second, followed by the need to set up a home and become socially established. A shared intimacy that includes sex gets relegated to something one maybe engages in just before retiring, if sleep doesn't take over first. Before long, lovemaking becomes an afterthought or obligation, rather than the ultimate rightful pleasure of two people who deeply care for one another.

In order to be lovers again and find the sexual happiness you are seeking, two important questions must be answered: How did you allow your mutual commitment to be lovers to drop to the bottom of your priorities list? How do you make your love for each other number one again? The first thing you want to consider is that you do have choices.

You can choose not to *over-schedule* activities for the children, and *schedule in* some activities for yourselves. The second thing you need to consider is that the better organized you are, the easier it will be to get your needs met. For example, if you cannot find a baby sitter for Friday night, don't give up. See if you can get a baby sitter for Saturday morning and take yourselves out for a quiet brunch.

MARITAL PRIORITY VS. MARITAL SACRIFICE

In our effort to be good parents, an interesting thing happens. We often become the people we do not really want to be, and obligate ourselves to duties we do not really want to perform. We sacrifice our identities and our marriages for the sake of our children to ensure their happiness, yet in reality, we make everyone miserable, particularly ourselves.

When parents become more committed to goals of obligation or achievement, instead of to each other, they become less directly involved in one another's lives. As this pattern continues, each spouse feels less cared for, less valued, less desired. "This is one of the main reasons why sex grows unsatisfactory," say Masters and Johnson. [3] And when the parents themselves do not feel valued or desired, it is much more difficult for them to help their children to feel valued and wanted.

Karen is a case in point. She was raising three children under age five, doing all the cooking, cleaning, changing diapers, wiping runny noses herself. She felt that as a stay-at-home mother, it was her duty to do everything herself. She grew tired and depressed "One day, my oldest child came up to me and asked, 'Mommy, why don't you smile anymore?' I knew something had to change," recalls Karen. "Suddenly, it dawned on me to get help."

Karen hired a teen-ager to come to her home from three o'clock in the afternoon until six o'clock in the evening, to feed the kids dinner and clean the kitchen so she could take a shower, relax and fix herself up before her husband came home from work. "It made all the difference in the world," she recalled. "I started smiling again."

In trying to be everything to everybody, it did not occur to Karen to hire someone to help her with the various household duties to relieve the stress she was feeling. Karen is a very intelligent woman and currently director of a parent support group organization. Her children have grown and are happy, healthy teen-agers. The problem Karen was experiencing was over-commitment to her family, which left her depleted of energy for herself and her husband.

> *"When you love your children—as all mothers start out doing—and you do your best—whatever that may be—the only failure is the failure on your part to maintain your own identity and to think of yourself first. The proverbial guilt trip, is something someone else has sold you."* [4]
> —Sanford J. Matthews, M.D., with Maryann Bucknum Brinley from *Through the Motherhood Maze: Survival Lessons for Loving Mothers. . . From an Outspoken Children's Doctor*

Mothers are particularly susceptible to the over-commitment syndrome, but fathers are, too. They tend to over-commit themselves to their work, stepping to the old beat of the father-as-breadwinner role. When they arrive home, they march to the beat of the father-as-nurturer role. It is all right to be a warm, loving, attentive father, but not to the point where you allow no time for yourself, or your spouse.

One father had bought season tickets to the ballet for himself and his wife. He thought it would be a nice way for them to have some time together, and to share an area of interest they both enjoyed. At the last minute, however, he began to feel guilty and bought a third ticket so his daughter could join them—a decision he now regrets. Since he gave up an opportunity to have some special time with his wife, he now seldom has any.

Many parents I interviewed felt that when their children were young, the children should come first. The idea being that there would be plenty of time later to pay attention to each other, when the kids were older. This is a big mistake. Couples with older children regretted the lost time, not to mention the lost intimacy. "It took us several years of the children coming first for us to realize that *we* had to come first, or our relationship was going to get lost in the shuffle," said Tammy, mother of three children, eight, six and three-and-a-half.

> *"As many marriages fail because of children as children fail because of faulty marriages. Until we learn that children are not special, but equal in importance to all of us, until we learn that we must not lead our lives and our marriages for children, but with them, we sacrifice our marriages, our own development."* [5]
>
> —Dr. Paul Pearsall, psychologist

In raising our children, we need to teach them that Mom and Dad need time alone together sometimes. Don't allow your unrealistic sense of duty to your children make you and your husband strangers to each other. It was just the two of you before your children were born. Hopefully, it will be just the two of you when your children leave home. If you don't have enough time with each other, it is because you don't *make* the time, and you don't *make* the time because you have allowed your guilty feelings to dictate to you how your time will be spent. If you don't have enough money to spend on the two of you for some activities you want to do together, then you have also allowed your feelings of guilt to dictate to you how your money will be spent. Spending time and money on yourselves is time and money *well spent*. It is an investment in your relationship, and in your family.

How do we, as parents, strike a happy balance and decide where our needs begin and our children's end? How do we fulfill those needs when our responsibilities seem so overwhelming? You begin to weigh these questions by acknowledging that you are lovers first, parents second.

"Generally, when couples discover, after a period of time, that they are acting more as business partners than married lovers, it comes as a bit of a shock and usually with considerable regret. Rarely do they understand what is happening. They have forgotten that before their marriage they were two people who tried to be together as much as they could because they found comfort and security in each other's acceptance, appreciation and understanding. This was the commitment of mutual concern. With marriage, however, they became husbands and wives, individuals who expected to take care of specialized responsibilities and who increasingly followed separate paths if their day's work was to be done. They slowly became emotionally uncommitted—and were left with the commitment of obligation." [2]

— Drs. William H. Masters and Virginia E. Johnson from their book, *The Pleasure Bond*

HOW TO GET THE HELP YOU NEED

- ♥ Ask neighbors and friends for names of teen-agers who would be willing to come to your home after school and lend a hand.

- ♥ Be sure to find a baby sitter who is interested enough to make the commitment to come to your home one or two days a week.

- ♥ See if you can develop a baby-sitting exchange with your neighbor, whereby you watch her children two days a week, then she watches your kids, so you can get errands run, or just take some relaxing time for yourself.

- ♥ Ask neighbors for names of teen-agers who would be interested in coming to your home on a Saturday to help you clean. Often if you both work, the house looks like a bomb hit it by the weekend.

- ♥ Get help from your children if they are old enough. If you don't feel you are getting the cooperation from them that you need, then sit down and have a family meeting and make up your own job chart, with specific duties assigned to each child. Have a Saturday clean-a-thon, and don't let anyone go anywhere until their specific jobs are done.

You have accepted the responsibilities of parenthood, but have a right to certain pleasures, too. The balance between your needs and your children's needs is ever changing, as you and your children are ever changing. If your children are sick, of course you take care of them first. However, not all responsibilities are set in stone. They can be negotiated between the two of you. If you feel your marriage is suffering beneath a tremendous weight of responsibilities, then step back and take a good hard look at whose needs are being sacrificed.

> *"Nothing has a stronger influence on children than the unlived life of the parents."* [6]
>
> —Carl Gustav Jung, psychiatrist

The happiest parents put their marriages first, and work to keep their relationship in the number one spot. They arranged time alone together during the week in the evenings, or in the mornings; and on the weekends they found a Friday or Saturday evening, or a Saturday or Sunday morning. They arranged to go away together for a weekend or a week at least once or twice a year. If you are having trouble arranging time alone with your spouse, or are not sure what you want to do with your time together, first schedule a meeting. Plan a time and place to meet where you will not be distracted by the children or telephone calls. If you are going to have any time together, you must plan for it.

Begin your meeting by thinking about the many ways you enjoy being together. Write down on separate pieces of paper your action activities, such as making love, dancing and playing tennis. Next, write down sedentary pleasures, such as taking a bath or listening to music. Jot down whatever delights come to mind. Don't let present obligations inhibit your brainstorming session.

Next, make a list on separate sheets of paper of specific, stimulating activities about making love that you enjoy, or would like to try, such as oral sex or making love in an unusual place.

Then, compare your lists. As you study one another's lists, you and your partner will develop a better understanding of each other's dreams and goals. The wish lists can be invaluable because they help you to focus your dreams, generate open conversation between the two of you about your desires, and put you on the right track to realizing them.

When you have done this, keep a daily record for the coming week of your schedules. You can chart your appointments and obligations on several sheets of paper or in a calendar book. Don't forget to plan time for your second meeting at the end of the week. During your second meeting, compare schedules and circle those moments you spent together. Study your charts and note where in your schedules your time was taken up with activities you elected to do, such as getting your hair cut; and where your time was taken up with regular responsibilities, such as coaching soccer on Wednesdays. Note also the time you spent doing something special for each other, which helps set the mood for sexual desire.

Now discuss which activities you could do together, change around or delete in order to have more priority time. Instead of going your separate ways to run errands on the weekends, could you do some of these errands together? It may take longer to do them, but at least you will be able to visit with each other. If you find yourselves rushing out the door every Saturday morning for Katy's gymnastic lesson, could you schedule it for during the week, so you and your husband could make love while Katy is busy watching television?

Scheduling a Vacation

If you have never taken a vacation alone together, or if the last time you spent any extended time away was on your honeymoon, pick a date on your calendar and make the arrangements to get away. Call baby-sitting agencies, your relatives if you have family living nearby or even your neighbors, and find a caretaker you feel you can trust, one with whom your children can become very familiar with before you leave. One couple I know, has a baby-sitting exchange with another couple. They take turns watching each other's children. The kids have a great time, and the parents get their much needed break.

In deciding when to leave for your vacation and how many days to spend away, you will need to consider your children's ages, their personalities and any stressful situations they may be experiencing. Going on a trip for one week or longer may be too stressful for most children four years old and younger. However, an overnight or weekend jaunt is certainly reasonable. Children age five and older are better able to handle longer absences from their parents of a week or two. If you have recently moved, or experienced a death in the family, if your child is starting a new summer camp or a new grade in

PREPARE YOUR CHILDREN FOR YOUR TRIP

♥ Plan your vacation at least three or four weeks in advance so your children will have plenty of time to get used to the idea of your leaving, and to the baby sitter coming.

♥ Explain to your children why it is important for the two of you to get away. One mother tells her children: "We want to be a strong family, and in order to do this, Mommy and Daddy have to have some time alone together."

♥ Talk a lot to your children about who will be taking care of them. It is a good idea to have this person baby-sit several times for short periods before you depart on your vacation.

♥ Plan special activities the children can do with their caretaker, and talk about these activities.

♥ Help small children visualize how long you will be gone, and reassure them of your return. You can make a large calendar with colorful stickers for the day you leave and the day you will be home. Then, each day, the child can put a new sticker in another box.

♥ Give your children photos of yourselves that they can hold and look at frequently. This can be reassuring. One friend of mine gives her kids photos, and also makes a tape recording of her voice and her husband's voice telling the children how much they love them, and that they will be home soon. If you want to get elaborate, you can make a video tape of yourselves.

♥ Telephone your children once you're away from home. Calling can help, but a word of caution here. If you tell your children you will call them at seven o'clock, be sure to stick to this time. Don't make a promise you won't be able to keep, because if your child sees he or she can't trust you to call, your child may feel he or she can't trust that you will return.

school, this would not be the best time to leave. If your child's environment is relatively stable, and *you* are the ones who can give the phrase "a bundle of nerves" new meaning, then take your vacation!

PREPARE YOUR SITTER FOR YOUR TRIP

♥ Leave the name and telephone number of where you will be staying, along with all important telephone numbers, such as police, fire department, the children's doctor, dentist, etc.

♥ Leave the names and telephone numbers of neighbors who may be contacted in case of an emergency.

♥ Don't forget to leave an extra house key with a neighbor just in case your baby sitter gets locked out of the house.

♥ Make a list of activities your baby sitter can do with the children, as well as meal suggestions, bedtime routines, forms of discipline, friends they can have over or are allowed to visit.

♥ Go over everything with the sitter about the house: how the locks work, how the burglar alarm works, what time the water sprinklers go on, where the fire extinguisher is and where the fuse box is.

♥ Tell the sitter where you keep your flashlights and candles just in case there is a blackout and where your earthquake survival kit is, if you have one. It is also a good idea to have a first-aid kit available and make sure the sitter can find it.

♥ Write down directions on how to get to your children's doctor's office, the dentist and the hospital, if the sitter is new to the area.

♥ Remember to leave the key to the car and all appropriate car insurance information if the baby sitter is going to be driving your car.

♥ Leave a medical permissions form, with all appropriate health insurance information in case your baby sitter needs to take your children to a doctor for medical attention. Include all appropriate health insurance policy information, and don't forget to indicate whether or not your children are allergic to any medications.

♥ Let your baby sitter know if you happen to change your plans and go to a different hotel or restaurant, other than the places you told your baby sitter you would be.

"Kids need to learn how to handle their parents' absence," relates Blake Rodgers, a marriage and family counselor in San Rafael, California. "The boundaries around the family can become too tight. Parents need to have room to move in and out of the family unit." Above all, keep reminding yourselves that it is all right to go away. A separation period of the right amount, at the right time, is healthy for everyone.

Points to Remember

1. Do not live your life *for* your children, but *with* them.

2. Teach your children that Mom and Dad need time alone once in a while. Don't allow your unrealistic sense of duty to your children make you and your spouse strangers to each other.

3. Spending some time and money on yourselves is time and money *well spent*. It is an investment in your relationship, and in your family.

4
Connect + Conquer

How to Keep Parenting from Destroying Your Sexual Desire

In any couple's travel down the road through parenthood, spouses must deal with tremendous life changes, their expectations and the realities of parenthood and the process of establishing priorities. They must also figure out how to raise best their child in order to help him or her grow into a physically and emotionally healthy human being, and how to create a happy family environment in which the two of them can keep their love intact. Even with all the helpful parenting advice available these days, the job of parenting is extremely difficult, although at times, incredibly rewarding. Dr. Benjamin Spock himself, admitted to having to seek the counsel of a family therapist when he and his second wife, Mary Morgan, were having difficulty with Mary's daughter Ginger accepting him, and with their ability to establish a happy, healthy stepfamily. So take heart in the fact that even if conflicts with raising your children appear to threaten your love for each other, there are solutions to problems and ways to keep you lovers.

> *"We parents so often blow the business of raising kids, but not*
> *because we violate any philosophy of child rearing. I doubt*
> *there can be a philosophy about something so difficult, some-*
> *thing so mystical, as raising kids."* [1]
> —Bill Cosby, actor and author

In talking with one father of a two-year-old daughter about how such difficulties as a child not wanting to go to sleep at night or waking up several times in the night interferes with one's desire for sex, he said, half-joking: "There is a direct correlation between conflict and the penis curve. As the conflict level rises, the penis curve drops; desire wanes."

Difficulties that parents have related to me that affect sexual desire range from children waking frequently in the night, to children being sick with colds or flu, to a lack of self-esteem, to discipline problems with stepchildren, to power struggles over which parent is right when dealing with a child's needs.

Unfortunately, children are not born with instruction manuals. Consequently, parents are in no way prepared for the feelings of fear, self-doubt, guilt, depression, resentment and anger they are *not* supposed to feel when their children come into the world, or are part of the package in a second marriage. Nor are parents prepared for these same feelings they may harbor toward their spouses.

A good example of this is the mother who has a baby who does not sleep through the night at three months of age, like many of the baby books tell her he or she should. In fact, she has been up four times in the night with this baby, while her husband has slept soundly. She adores her baby boy, but is very upset at him and wonders if she is not doing something she *should* be because the baby is not sleeping. She is so angry at her spouse that he is getting a good night's sleep while she is not, that making love is the last thing on her mind. "What *sex*? When the baby finally dozed off, I got back into bed and kicked my husband!" one mother told me.

I don't advocate kicking your husband. Feeling good about ourselves and each other enough to get turned on is a matter of understanding and learning how to manage the conflicts that do arise in parenting our children. Through my research in writing this book, I have found parents who are willing to share their difficulties, explain how these difficulties interfered with their sexual desire and tell what they did about these stressful situations. Children's sleeping problems, illnesses, discipline troubles and power struggles can often upset the best of plans, but they can be successfully managed.

SOME COMMON SLEEPING PROBLEMS

Children who resist going to bed, who wake up several times in the night as a result of bedtime fears and anxieties or who have sleep terrors or nightmares, constitute some of the common situations parents must deal with.

It is normal for children to awaken two or three times in the night to be fed during the first three or four months of their lives. However, if they are continuing to wake up frequently after four months, and certainly after six months and are otherwise healthy, this is something you can gradually work on changing. Of course, this varies from child to child. Nursing infants digest breast milk more quickly than formula and therefore might wake up more often. If you are having trouble with your child's frequent nighttime waking, I recommend that you read *Nighttime Parenting* by Dr. William Sears (New American Library, 1987) and of course, consult your doctor.

> *"These periods of 'unnecessary hunger' at night are an outgrowth of periods of 'necessary hunger' that are present in the smaller infant. . . If your child has grown accustomed to having a significant amount of his daily calories at night, he can easily learn to transfer this caloric intake into the daytime. It is not difficult for your child to change the times at which he becomes hungry, but again it is up to you. . . If you change his routines in favor of daytime feedings only, he will soon change his hunger patterns accordingly and his nutritional needs will still be met."* [2]
>
> —Dr. Richard Ferber, a pediatrician and author of
> *Solve Your Child's Sleep Problems*

Bedtime Resistance

Something as simple as the change in a child's daytime routine can wreak havoc on a couple's relationship.

"We had a terrible problem when my daughter Erin started pre-school and her naptime changed from eleven o'clock in the morning to two o'clock in the afternoon," relates Gina, the mother of a two-and-a-half-year-old. "In the evenings, she would be awake until eleven o'clock at night. Sometimes we would let her watch television with us. Sometimes we would spend our entire evening putting her back in her crib. One night, we put her in her crib fifteen times and she climbed out fifteen times. We finally put up a kiddie gate in her bedroom doorway and she climbed over that! My husband and I could not make love, or even go to sleep when we wanted to. This went on for close to six months!

"My husband finally got the idea to put up two kiddie gates, one on top of the other in the doorway, and that did the trick. She could still see out and take comfort in the fact that we were nearby, but also learn that when the kiddie gates go up, it's time for bed. It took us several nights of putting up the kiddie gates, but now she usually goes to sleep by nine o'clock, without the kiddie gates. She has also learned to play in her room if she's not tired, then go to sleep."

Erin's bedtime routine had obviously changed because of her change in the naptime schedule. As Dr. Ferber points out, you cannot make your children fall asleep earlier at night if their routine has been upset, but you can wake them up earlier in the morning, and eventually make it possible for them to fall asleep earlier at night. One thing that is helpful for parents to realize is that some difficulties are not "just a stage" children go through and that you have to "wait it out." You can do something about situations that upset you.

Sleep Terrors

When children wake frequently in the night or have trouble going to sleep because of fears or anxieties, it is often helpful not only to look at outside issues, for example fears of a school bully, but also to explore tense situations within the home.

Robin and Jake have two children, Jessie, eight, and Annie, five, both of whom had begun to have erratic sleeping habits. "Each child began waking up two or three times in the night, every night, and this went on for months," says Robin. "On one occasion, the night before I took my accounting final, Jessie woke up five times and this was not from illness. If my husband and I hopped into bed with the intention of a roll in the hay, it wasn't that we gave up because we had one ear on the door, listening for the patter of little feet. It was that we were both totally exhausted."

In the case of Annie and Jessie, both girls were having trouble sleeping because they were intensely anxious and worried about their parents. Robin and Jake were in the process of having a new home built, one Jake wanted badly, but something Robin did not want at all. There was much anger between them, which created a tense environment. The frequent arguments and yelling caused the children to be frightened and worried. It was only when Robin and Jake saw a marriage counselor and worked through the tensions of their power struggle, of which the new house was only part of the issue, that things settled down with the children.

If you are faced with a sleep terror, it is helpful to be near your child, but try not to wake him or her up. A sleep terror is not the same as a nightmare and can take on many forms. It is a partial awakening from the deepest phase of non-dreaming, non-REM sleep. Usually, during this phase the child may mumble, turn over and then go back into another deep sleep cycle. Sometimes, this transition between sleep stages may become extended, and the child may thrash about or cry or scream, which may seem similar to a temper tantrum. Also he or she may walk around the crib or get out of the crib or bed and start walking.

During a sleep terror, the child usually has a glassy look in his eyes, acts like he does not know you and may not want to be touched. In fact, if you try to comfort him, he may push you away and act more upset. It is usually best to let the child alone, except for making sure he does not hurt himself. Move toys out of his or her crib or off the floor. Sleep terrors usually last from fifteen to forty-five minutes. The child falls back into a deep sleep and remembers nothing about what happened.

The best way to help avoid sleep terrors is to make sure your child gets enough sleep and that his or her schedule is regular and consistent. Above all, don't panic and start blaming each other. Keep in mind that you are on the same team. If you and your spouse feel frightened at watching your child experience a sleep terror, instead of standing there feeling helpless, hold each other. This is what my husband and I did when our younger daughter experienced some sleep terrors. We were far more frightened than she was. In fact, the next morning when she woke up, she was her usual jolly self, unaware of her sleep terror. Something else you don't want to do is scare your child unnecessarily, so it is best not to mention the sleep terror to him or her.

Nightmares

Nightmares can also be disturbing to parents, as they try to find out what frightened or worried their child enough to cause them. All children have nightmares from time to time. Although some nightmares occur with high fever or are a side effect of certain medications, according to Dr. Ferber, most are psychological in nature and reflect the same type of anxieties that cause a child to be too scared to go to bed at night. If your child is two or three you may be able to find out what his or her fear is by talking to him or her. If your child is an adolescent, he or she will recognize that it was a nightmare, and may want to talk to you about it, or just go back to sleep, feeling reassured that you are nearby. A toddler, however, has trouble distinguishing dreams from reality, and is just as frightened as if the dreams had really happened. Telling him or her it was "just a dream" is not going to help alleviate the toddler's fear. Says Ferber: "Here is one time your child really needs your presence at night. . . it is a time to be lenient and loving, to say, 'I'm here as long as you need me.' " [3]

If your child continues night after night to be too frightened to go to sleep, or has frequent sleep terrors or nightmares, try to discover what the trouble is and seek professional help if necessary. As I mentioned, sometimes a child's sleep problem is a symptom of a greater problem in the home that needs to be resolved.

If a child is truly frightened, he or she will look it. If your child is merely testing you, he or she will walk calmly, and talk calmly about monsters or ghosts. Sometimes children talk about monsters as a way to "test their limits," in order to stay up and watch television, or as an excuse to sleep in their parents' bed. Sometimes they are just not sleepy yet, and bombard their parents with excuses. If their monster story works, they will keep using it. Be firm and set limits.

"When I was a kid, I used to imagine animals running under my bed. I told my dad and he solved the problem quickly. He cut the legs off the bed." [4]

—Lou Brock, ex-baseball player

Other Problems

Several parents I've talked with said their evenings for any kind of togetherness, whether this meant holding hands, kissing while watching television or having sexual intercourse, were totally thrown off by something as simple as daylight saving time.

"Trying to get the kids to bed by eight o'clock in the summertime when it's still daylight takes an enormous effort," relates Susan, mother of two daughters, four and seven. "I'm forty-four years old and am very energetic, but if I don't get my children to bed by eight o'clock at night, I begin to tire out and the time after this is bad for all of us. I don't like my kids and they don't like me. My husband and I get cross with each other, and any desire for sex goes right out the window. I often tell myself that I am preserving all of our relationships by getting my children to bed before I get miserable."

A major breakthrough in understanding and treating sleep problems came when researchers began to see that sleep and waking is a rhythm that has to act in harmony with other body rhythms, such as body temperature, eating, hormone release and activity. "If we are to sleep well and function at our best during the day, these biological rhythms have to be smoothly synchronized," says Dr. Ferber. [5] In light of this discovery, it is easy to see how something like daylight saving time can interfere with a child's ability to go to sleep when a child's parents want him or her to. It is springtime or summertime. The temperature is warmer. It is obviously lighter at night. There is a tendency to eat dinner later. And to let kids sleep later in the morning if school is over for the school year.

If you find that daylight saving time has caused trouble with getting your kids to bed, consider your daily schedule. If you have started eating dinner later, move the dinner hour back to where it was during the wintertime. If you have allowed your children to sleep late, wake them up an hour earlier, so they will be ready to go to bed an hour earlier at night, which will actually be the same time they went to bed *before* daylight saving time. If light in the bedroom is making it hard for your kids to sleep, consider putting up blackout shades, or perhaps heavier curtains. These will help to cut out light and even some summertime noise. Hopefully, your kids will be less inclined to peek out the window to see what is going on in the neighborhood.

CHILDREN'S AILMENTS

Sometimes, when we least expect it, children get sick or have some physical problem that taps all the love and energy and concern we have to give, so that our own desires and needs get put on the back burner temporarily. Our children need us, so we go to them. And it is only when we feel they are well and safe that we can allow ourselves to indulge our needs. This is part of parenthood. Fortunately, for most of us, our children are not sick all the time.

Your Handicapped Child

For those parents who have a handicapped child, it is necessary to address any and all feelings that you may have. If necessary, seek some form of counseling to help you heal your relationship if it is floundering. It is also important to make some time for yourselves, even if it means finding a qualified baby sitter and having her watch your child while you have some time together at home. According to pediatrician Charlotte Thompson, author of *Raising a Handicapped Child* (Ballentine, 1987), there is a tendency for parents of a handicapped child to blame each other, particularly if the cause of the handicap was due to a hereditary factor. There is also a tendency for the mother to commit so much time to her handicapped child, that the father feels neglected. The financial stress of caring for a handicapped child is also greater, which creates an additional burden on the couple and their relationship.

Dr. Charlotte Thompson, who is the director of the Center of Handicapped Children and Teen-Agers in San Francisco, urges those parents to: "Find ways to pay attention to your own lives. Make a date once a week, but don't talk about your problems." She also suggests that parents might benefit from being involved in a support group for parents of handicapped kids. Sometimes, if the parents are reluctant to have a baby sitter watch their child, they may be able to find other parents who have a child with the same handicap, with whom they can trade off baby-sitting services.

The Common Cold to Chicken Pox

Caring for children with a handicap is hard. Caring for children who get hit with the common illnesses such as colds, flu and chicken pox is also stressful and can put strains on a couple's relationship. However, stresses and disappointments can be made less difficult if you don't allow your love to get lost in the shuffle.

"One night, my husband and I were in the middle of making love and Joni, my youngest, who was eight years old at the time, walked in on us when our door was shut," recalls Jill, mother of four children ranging in age from twelve to eighteen. "She knew that when our door is closed you don't come in unless there is an emergency, and even then, you knock. She was sick with the flu, and figured she was going to come in no matter what. My husband and I quickly got dressed and took care of her, but we also made a date for ourselves to make love the following night."

If your lovemaking is interrupted by a child's illness, don't give up and let this be a time to forget each other. Your children need you to be with them, but you can still find ways to feel connected to your spouse. For example, when you go to the drug store to buy medicines, buy five or ten cards to have on hand to send to your spouse at his or her office, or put on the dresser at home during those difficult times. Buy funny or sexy cards, whatever suits your style. You don't have to spend a long time picking them out. Just quickly choose several cards, so that when times are rough, you can take two minutes to say, "I Love You!" with a card. And, of course, when you finally do have time to talk, make a sex date, so you can pick up where you left off. Often, just giving each other a hug can help you to cope better with tough times.

Larry and Donna found that just as they were getting in the mood for sex and ready to go to bed, their eleven-month-old baby, Dale, would wake up crying from teething pain. "It never failed, for two weeks in a row, precisely at eleven o'clock, he would wake up," relates Larry. "I'd be all excited about getting it on with Donna, then whammo, forget sex! We decided the only way we were going to have time for each other was to set our alarm clock for six o'clock, and make love in the morning, which we did."

This is a good, practical solution for a weekend, because then you can take turns watching the baby, so each of you gets a chance to take a nap. You can also hire a baby sitter to take the baby for a walk, or trade baby-sitting times with a neighbor (you watch my kid, then I'll watch yours), so you and your spouse have some time to make love without being disturbed.

Kyle and Dana had planned a twelfth wedding anniversary trip to St. Thomas, in the Virgin Islands, something they had been looking forward to for a long time. They had hired a baby sitter to care for their two sons, Danny and Jeff, eight and six. Two days before they were supposed to leave, Danny came down with chicken pox. "We had to cancel our trip and were really disappointed," said Dana. "We had fantasies of making love on a tropical island. But when we called to tell our baby sitter we couldn't go, we checked with her about some future dates, and figured out another week on the calendar when we could take our vacation. It helped a lot, knowing we still had a date to celebrate our anniversary."

When children get sick, sometimes special vacations have to be canceled. This does not mean, however, that you cannot schedule another time to be together. In other words, don't pull out all the stops, until you have considered all the angles.

SEX AND SELF-ESTEEM

A desire for sex, or feeling desirable, has a great deal to do with our feelings of self-worth. This is particularly true for women whose feelings of self-esteem are tied very closely to their role as mothers. If they feel good about the role itself and competent in their ability to parent, they are more likely to feel good about themselves in the bedroom. If they feel ill-equipped to handle their children due to a lack of parenting skills, because they are going through an especially difficult period with their children or because they have not taken off any time to nurture themselves, this can take its toll on sexual desire.

Rob and Jane, who have two children, Todd, four, and Heather, one, had not had sexual intercourse for a period of six months due to Jane's extreme lack of self-esteem. "I was a CPA in public accounting before I had children," says Jane. "I was promoted frequently and made a lot of money at a young age. I thought I was hot stuff, then when I quit working to raise a family, I began to feel terrible. Even though I knew what I wanted to do was be with my kids, when I became a mother, all of a sudden I felt like a nothing. As a mother, I wasn't getting a bonus check, a promotion or all those pats on the back you get when you are working in a paying job. There is just not

---

FEEL GOOD ABOUT BEING A MOM

♥ Do something fun for yourself at least once a week, whether you spend your days at the office or at home. Go to the gym, take yourself out to lunch or get a manicure.

♥ Look into doing some volunteer or part-time work if you find yourself missing your old job. Find something that you can fit into *your* schedule, not the other way around.

♥ Look into joining a parent support group, where you can not only meet other mothers but find playmates for your kids.

♥ Talk to the director of your parent support group about parenting classes you might sign up for to learn some helpful parenting skills, if you are not feeling very effective in your efforts to discipline your children.

♥ Look into finding a qualified therapist you feel comfortable with— someone who can help you to deal with your depression and feel good about yourself again, if after making some effort to help yourself, you still feel depressed. The American Association of Sex Educators, Counselors and Therapists offers listings for certified sex therapists nationwide (312) 644-0828.

---

much respect given to people who do what I'm doing, which is raising children. This really affected me."

Jane felt guilty about hiring a baby sitter so she could take some time off. She also felt guilty about spending any money on herself because she was no longer bringing in a paycheck. Through counseling, she was able to understand how she was jeopardizing her own sense of self-worth by denying her own needs or always putting them last. In discussing the anger, resentment and frustration she felt at not getting her own needs met, she began to realize that her needs were important. By nurturing herself, she began to feel better about herself, and more confident as a parent. Jane and Rob are continuing to work through their sexual difficulties, and sex for them has become a reality again.

When one spouse is unhappy as a result of unfulfilled needs, there is a ripple effect. The other spouse is affected, and the relationship is affected. When resentments and misunderstandings are allowed to fester, and when needs go unexpressed, sexual and marital unhappiness is the result.

Some therapists estimate that anywhere from twenty to fifty percent of the general population may experience Inhibited Sexual Desire (ISD) at some time in their lives, to some degree. A few therapists estimate the figure to be as high as eighty percent. Researchers who have conducted research on ISD have discovered "Marital unhappiness is one of the most frequent causes of inhibited desire." [6] According to noted psychiatrist Helen Singer Kaplan, who brought wide attention to this problem in 1979, "People who suffer from ISD may have a normal sexual impulse, but a 'turn-off' mechanism, such as anger or anxiety squelches it." [7]

If you are carrying a heavy burden of anger and guilt, you don't have to. Talk to your spouse about your needs. Discuss what it is that is making you so unhappy, and talk about what you can do to make yourself happy.

BEING LOVERS IN A STEPFAMILY

Trying to stay lovers in the midst of all the difficulties that come up is hard. Trying to stay lovers in a stepfamily is even harder.

When Diane married Joe four years ago, she became stepmother to his six-year-old daughter Stephanie and fourteen-month-old son Jason. Joe became stepfather to Diane's two-year-old son Ryan. Before they had married, Joe had sole custody of his two children and had been taking care of them with the help of his mother, the children's grandmother. Stephanie had grown very close to her father, and had, in a sense, taken it upon herself to play "the little mother" role. When Joe married Diane, Stephanie was not at all happy. She greatly resented Diane, and did everything she could to make life miserable for her.

"Stephanie would not listen to anything I said, and would constantly boss her brother and stepbrother around. She would always tell me that I wasn't raising them right. We would get into some terrible arguments, and by the end of the day, I would feel so angry and frustrated that I would scream at Joe as soon as he came home from work. The tension level in our home was so high, that whenever I could get any time to myself, I just wanted to escape into the bedroom and let my mind rest. I didn't want to think about anything, especially sex."

As Dr. Spock points out, from his own experience: "It's important for stepparents to realize that, to a child, the re-marriage of a parent is the final severing of the original, intact family. As a result, even if you came along ten years after the death or divorce of her biological parent, irrationally, she probably sees you as standing in the way of her parents being together." [8]

This is a rather complex issue because the child feels terrible resentment and anger, but underneath these feelings is the great sadness the child feels because his or her parents will never get back together. A child also may experience fear that the parent that has re-married will abandon him or her, as the other parent may have done. In Stephanie's case, her mother was a drug addict and did not want to have anything to do with her children. Stephanie had become very close to her father, whom she greatly feared she would lose to Diane. And even though her mother had abandoned her, she felt she had to be loyal to her. Any affection she may have wanted to show Diane would have meant, in her mind, that she was being disloyal to her mother. Add to this Diane's fears of losing Joe because of conflicts with Stephanie and Joe's frustration of feeling like he had to try constantly to find ways to make his daughter and wife like each other and not succeeding at all, and you have not only family unhappiness, but a great deal of marital unhappiness.

"It was real tough on me," recalled Joe. "Here I was, trying to take good care of my family, and I wasn't getting any sex, or even much affection from Diane. I kept asking myself, 'What did I do to deserve *this*?' It was real frustrating to be laying in bed with Diane, rubbing her back, knowing that the minute my penis started to get hard, she was going to roll over and go to sleep."

After some discussion, Diane, Joe and Stephanie went to see a family counselor to talk about their feelings of anger, resentment and fear. In expressing their true feelings, they were better able to understand how natural and inevitable their feelings were, and learn how to deal with them. "I learned that I had to stop trying so hard to make Diane and Stephanie like each other, and let them develop a relationship on their own," related Joe. For Diane, forming a relationship with Stephanie took several months, but she found that talking to Stephanie about her feelings, and allowing Stephanie a chance to express her thoughts, eased the tension quite a bit. If Stephanie felt uncomfortable talking to Diane, Joe made sure he was available to talk. As for Joe and Diane's relationship, they realized that in order to stay united as a couple, they would have to develop one way of dealing with all disciplinary problems and decisions affecting the family. In other words, they would have to form a united front, and not allow Stephanie to play them off one another. Gradually, over time, as Joe and Diane strengthened their relationship by talking about their feelings and making decisions together, their stepfamily grew stronger, too.

"All of us are much more relaxed with each other now," said Diane. "The stress level has greatly decreased, and I am gaining more confidence in myself as a stepparent. Things are getting better sexually, too. My sexual desire is coming back."

Realistic Ways to Solve Stepparenting Problems

You need to realize that any antagonism your stepchild may feel toward you is not a personal attack. It is a normal reaction to the intrusion of an outsider into the intimacy of his or her original family. You shouldn't try to compete with the absent parent, or insist that the child call you Dad or Mom. Perhaps you can decide together how your stepchild should address you.

Although as lovers, it may be hard to keep your hands off each other, go slowly in showing a lot of open affection for a while, as this might cause the child to show more hostility toward the stepparent and parent. Many children never give up their dream that one day their parents will get back together, so they may see that any affection is a sign of unfaithfulness on the parent's part.

Also, try to understand that jealousy toward a stepparent is a natural reaction, and best handled by openly recognizing this feeling and allowing your child to talk about it. You might say: "I know you sometimes feel jealous and angry about Nancy. You want Daddy all to yourself." You need to allow your child to have his or her angry or jealous feelings. Instead of causing more tension, the expressing of feelings helps to diffuse it.

While it is important that you allow your child to express his or her feelings, this does not mean that you, and your new wife or husband have to take abuse from the child. You have a right to your love, and you do not have to apologize, or "make it up" to your child for being together. Your child's rudeness should not be tolerated. So rather than criticizing the child or punishing him or her, try to share your honest feelings. Sometimes a child's rudeness or coldness is a result of his or her feeling that if he or she shows any affection toward the stepparent that this means he or she is being disloyal to the absent parent. Reassuring him or her that you have no intention of taking the absent parent's place, but that you just want to be friends, may help.

In the area of discipline, often stepparents experience a double whammy. They bring into a new relationship their backgrounds on the way they were raised, plus a set way they may have been disciplining their children before forming a stepfamily. If one spouse has a different way of disciplining than the other, this causes another conflict. So, it is vital that you talk with each other about how you plan to discipline your children in your new family. You and your spouse should decide on a mutually agreeable plan, so your children don't divide you on issues.

In discussing family issues, you can't expect yourselves or each other to feel the same way toward your stepchildren as you feel toward your own children. You naturally have deeper feelings toward your own children and you don't have to feel guilty about it. You and your spouse should always try, however, to be fair, and not to lash out at your spouse and his or her child. Try to consider your spouse's point of view and his or her child's point of view and discuss issues and feelings openly.

When you and your spouse are making plans for the family, remember to schedule some quality time with your natural children and your stepchildren. They each need some of your undivided attention. Most importantly, spend some quality time with your spouse. It is easier in a stepfamily to allow feelings of guilt to interfere with making some time to be together, but taking the time to be lovers will strengthen your bond and better enable you to deal with family stresses.

Above all, you and your spouse should strive to be open with each other and to talk about your feelings. Some stepfamilies, for example, have weekly meetings where they come together and air gripes. A good approach to help you get the ball rolling is to say: "I know this is new for all of us, and it will take time for us to resolve our differences, share our values and handle responsibility."

If difficulties persist, you and your family may want to consult with a family therapist who specializes in stepfamily problems. Spouses have also reported that they are able to find much help and relief from tensions by joining a stepfamily support group. If you are interested in finding out about a group like this or obtaining more helpful information, contact The Stepfamily Association of America, 602 East Joppa Road, Baltimore, Maryland 21204, (301) 823-7570.

DISCIPLINE AND POWER STRUGGLES

In parenting, disagreements over disciplining the children is perhaps the biggest source of contention in many homes. Disagreements over deciding "what is best for the child" ran a close second. Almost every couple who answered my questionnaire felt that the tensions connected to discipline problems and the power struggles of making decisions regarding the well-being of the child, were the main killers of sexual desire. It is easy to see why. When couples marry, they bring into their relationship their backgrounds and the way they were raised. The way that they were disciplined may be different. Their values may be different. In their efforts to raise their own children, there are bound to be clashes and power struggles over whose method is right, or who is *the* parent in control.

In addition, it is no secret that children will test their parents constantly, and often try to pit parents against each other. One night, for example, a young father was getting his three-year-old son ready for a bath. Suddenly, the father became disgusted and marched out of the bathroom into the living room to see his wife. "You *know*, our son just peed in the bath tub and he said that you said it was OK!" The mother thought that this behavior was no big deal, which made the father more furious. The couple began arguing over who was right, and blew any thought of having sex after their son went to bed "right out of the water," figuratively speaking. Parents should calmly resolve such conflicts privately, if possible, and return to the child united. Resolution can lead to good sex, too.

The younger years can be frustrating as we try to teach our children proper behavior, in essence, civilize them. Then the adolescent years come along, which can be especially trying because children in their teens are so needy emotionally, as they struggle to discover who they are and how to deal with various peer pressures. They need you, yet at the same time, they don't want you to think they need you. "This testing process is part of their breaking away, of growing up, and you try to be understanding," explains Sally, the mother of three teen-agers. "At the same time, you can be so pissed off at them that you don't want anyone to touch you, including your husband. It does have an effect on your relationship."

Sometimes, just the minor discipline problem of a child lying, can be devastating to parents. It can stir up an argument between husband and wife, and push aside any desire for physical touching. "My wife came to me and told me our seven-year-old daughter Elyse had looked her straight in the eye and told her a lie," related Jim. "She was crushed, but I thought, 'What's the big deal?' This is something children do. You just have to discuss the problem and teach children right from wrong." But Jim's wife Donna became enraged at him because she felt he was not showing enough concern for Elyse. "I told her, 'You ought to let go of your anger,' " said Jim. "She blurted back, 'Don't tell me what to do!' Pretty soon, the argument we were having over who was more concerned about Elyse, had taken precedence over the lying incident."

> *"In a two-parent family, children must perceive that both their parents are united in their efforts to raise them. It is impossible to expect two different adults to agree on procedures and techniques for child rearing; however, parents must be mature enough to reach some common agreement as to their philosophies of behavior management."* [9]
> —Marvin Silverman, Ed.D., and David A. Lustig, Ph.D.,
>   in their book, *Parent Survival Training: A Complete Guide to Modern Parenting*

In Jim and Donna's situation, it might have been helpful at the moment for them briefly to excuse themselves from Elyse's presence, and have their argument in private. Often, when children witness their parents arguing in front of them, that just gives them more ammunition to drive a wedge between their parents. The last thing you want to do is give your child "manipulation power." If Donna and Jim still could not agree on a permanent course of action, they could agree on a temporary course of action, then come back and present a united front for Elyse. Donna and Jim would greatly benefit from having some quiet time together to delve into the various discipline issues that concern them, and reach a common agreement as to how they are going to deal with them.

> *"We each have our own perspective and we are each right to a certain degree. The goal of a satisfying relationship, however, is not to win by making our partner lose, but rather to work out problems so that both of us are satisfied. This is not always easy, or even possible under certain circumstances. But it is more possible if both people recognize it as the goal."* [10]
> —Lonnie Barbach, Ph.D., psychologist and sex therapist

"My son had a dreadful teacher and this caused him to dislike school," related Patti. "He would be in tears, complaining of headaches and stomachaches every morning. My husband and I had conferences with his teacher, the principal and a learning resource specialist. I wanted to ask for a teacher change, but my husband didn't agree. It was not the school issue that upset me so much. It was the issue of who was in power in our relationship, who makes the important decisions. I wanted Robert's support in stampeding the school system into handling the situation my way, but he did not share my point of view."

Patti's sexual desire for her husband didn't completely disappear during this difficult time, but it did decline. "Certainly, when you are angry with someone, it is not possible to have a warm, sexual relationship."

Robert felt that he and his wife should try to solve the difficulties with his son's teacher. Patti, however, felt that their son would be better off with a different teacher. One way that helped them solve their dilemma was to write down on a piece of paper all the reasons for their opinion about what to do to help their son. After writing down their reasons, they compared notes and talked. Patti listened quietly while Robert discussed his reasons, then Robert listened quietly while Patti discussed her reasons. They both tried to be empathetic and understanding. By not blaming each other, but listening with open minds, they were able find a solution. "While we both had good reasons, in the end we were able to see what was really best for our son, and that was to allow him to change to a different teacher," explained Patti.

BREAK THE POWER STRUGGLE GRIDLOCK!

♥ Separate and write down your thoughts and reasons for your opinion on a piece of paper, instead of arguing and yelling at each other.

♥ Set a time to get together after you both have had a chance to cool off and think. Try to find a quiet place to discuss your differences where you won't be distracted by the television or your children.

♥ Take turns going over your list of reasons and give each other a chance to air feelings and thoughts. When discussing the issues, try to focus on what issue is really the most important. Remember: No one wins if the goal is to prove who is right or wrong. Your ultimate goal is to work out problems.

When Kari's eighteen-year-old daughter Vanessa announced that she was going to be a nanny for a family in New York City for the entire summer, Kari was shocked. "It just blew me away," remembers Kari, who lives in Seattle, Washington. Kari's husband Brent felt Vanessa should be allowed to go in order for her to gain some autonomy. But Kari had a hard time feeling the same way.

"It was easier for Brent to see that her leaving was a very important step toward gaining independence. On a logical level, I knew this, but on an emotional level, I felt I was being robbed of my child," explained Kari. "When our son died several years ago, Vanessa was very close to me. She was home with me and was my whole support system. I just felt like someone was stealing her away."

In the end, Kari let Vanessa go, but not without becoming embroiled in several heated arguments with her husband Brent. Their anger against each other spoiled any sexual encounters they might have had with each other for several weeks. "Both of us have a very strong physical need. We are just that way," says Kari. "If we go more than two or three days without having sex, unless one of us is sick, then something is seriously wrong. We have usually been good about talking, though. While I knew Brent and Vanessa were right, I needed time to get used to the idea of her growing up, and to recognize that my anger was really a cover-up for my deeper feelings of sadness. Brent is a good listener and allowed me to express my feelings without judging me or ridiculing me. He realized that I just needed some time and space."

Sometimes, when arguments develop over issues, power struggles can't be resolved right away. One or both spouses need some time alone to think. In fact, sometimes, spouses put more importance on specific issues than is necessary, and arguments may be an indication that both spouses need some self time to get some perspective on their relationship. If this is the case for you, give each other some space.

One couple I interviewed had some very interesting solutions. When Suzanne and Jerry, parents of Jamie, twelve, and Tony, ten, become so angry with each other they cannot talk, they try to organize cooling off periods. "We both own the rocking chairs we had as infants, and when one person has calmed down enough to initiate discussion, he or she will sit in one of the rocking chairs," explains Suzanne. "The other person, seeing this, knows it is time to talk. We also both feel it is not terrible to apologize. We will often put our hands on each other's shoulders and say, 'Can we try again?' We also use a sense of humor. My husband and I took a mask-making course once. Sometimes, when I am in a rotten mood, I'll put on my ugly mask and he knows not to come near me."

TOO MUCH NOISE!

Many parents often have the most trouble when dealing with the noise children make and the irritating things that they do. Frequent noise and irritations can put us in a bad mood, and kill any inclinations for sex with our spouse. Some reported noise situations that bothered parents included the high-pitched crying of infants, fighting among siblings and the general rowdiness of children's play. Some reported irritations that drove parents crazy involved wet toilet paper wads stuck on the bathroom mirror, spoiled food under the bed and scattered toys with lost parts never to be found again.

"I came home from work one evening in a particularly good mood, and the first thing I did was hug my wife," related Tom, father of Brad, a precocious eight-year-old. "We were hugging and feeling real good about each other, when suddenly, we felt this water all over us. My son was squirting us with his squirt gun!"

THOUGHTFUL WAYS TO MAKE UP AFTER A FIGHT

♥ Apologize with a love note and give it to your spouse if you can't quite get up the nerve to talk yet.

♥ Call your spouse at the office. Sometimes putting a little distance between you by talking on the telephone, instead of in person, helps to mend hurt feelings.

♥ Make a special dinner at home, consisting of your favorite wine and foods that you both enjoy. You can do this with your children joining you, or wait until after they go to bed if they are younger. Sometimes, making up in front of the children is a good way for them to see that Mom and Dad get mad, but they still love each other; and that it is all right to get mad at the people you love. *All feelings are a part of who we are as people, and mad or sad feelings are not bad feelings.*

♥ Decide on a special word you can say to each other when you are ready to make up. My husband and I use the word "college," because we met and fell in love at college. This word not only lets the other person know that we are ready to make peace, it also stirs up those wonderful memories of when we first fell in love.

♥ Hug your spouse and say, "I'm sorry we had such a terrible fight." This is not the same thing as admitting you are wrong. It is a way to break the ice. If you are wrong, however, then apologize. Don't allow foolish pride to stand in the way of solving your problem.

Another father was incredibly irritated by all the commotion his two children made. Mark, father of Katie, five, and Steven, eight, had come from a small family where a lot of the usual noise children make was not permitted. Consequently, noise really bothers him. His wife Jan had come from a large family and is accustomed to noise. Together, however, they had to find a way to help Mark feel relaxed.

"It was a temperament issue," related Jan. "Noise exhausts Mark. It wasn't as if he sat down and said to himself, 'Well, how can I avoid being intimate? I know. I'll get the kids to yell and that will solve the problem.' Children fight with one another. You can live with it or minimize it. We designed some solutions, but they have to be planned. We trade off baby-sitting the kids on the weekend so Mark can have some time by himself. We try to keep the children separated to a large degree, and will often each take a child to a separate activity. As a couple, we create a quiet environment for ourselves by spending some weekends away at a friend's house on Martha's Vineyard, a small island in New England, where there are no telephones, no televisions or radios and no screaming kids."

SIMPLE WAYS TO EASE THE STRESS AT HOME

♥ Organize a "quiet time" in your home if your children are three years old or older. This is a time when children can quietly look at books or play board games or rest while listening to soft music—just like they do in nursery school! Forty-five minutes to an hour of peace and quiet will give you a chance to recharge your batteries.

♥ Avoid the mad dinner rush! When you both come home from working and picking up the kids at day care, or your day has been hectic at home, and you are waiting for your spouse to arrive, don't knock yourself out to have dinner on the table right away. Give the kids a snack. Give yourselves a snack. Kick off your shoes and take a half-hour break. You will be less crazed, and the dinner hour will be more enjoyable.

♥ Take turns allowing each other to sleep late one morning on the weekend. One wife I spoke to takes the kids out for breakfast on Saturday so her husband can sleep in. The following Saturday, he does the same for her.

♥ Have your husband take your child for a walk in the stroller, if he or she is a baby, so you can sleep in or take a nap. Then you do the same for him.

♥ Try something different when the children fall asleep. Instead of plopping down in front of the television set, take your coffee and go sit on your back porch if it is a moonlit night. If it is a chilly night, just bundle up and go out there anyway. Afterwards, come in and take a warm shower together.

CONTROL YOUR MOOD FOR SEX

At times, parents may feel they have no control over their situation. If a conflict arises, they may fly into a rage and let the consequences be what they will be. But you *do* have choices of action, and how you decide to act can either enhance a sexual mood or kill it. For example, when you are hugging your spouse, and your son decides to break up your embrace with a squirt-gun blast of water in your face, you can control the outcome of the situation and your mood. You can either scream at your child, which may encourage him to fire again and make you angrier. Or you can tell him calmly how this attack makes you feel, and put him and the gun on time out. Or you can laugh, squirt him back and tell him Mommy and Daddy need some time to hug. Then, both of you can pick up where you left off—hugging and kissing and thinking about sex.

Sex Is an Attitude

Sexual desire is a mysterious thing. There are many causes for a lack of libido, ranging from physical to environmental to emotional. Sexual desire also has a great deal to do with our *attitude*, with our ability to *make decisions*. We *choose* to love the person we love. Yes, we "fell in love" and experienced that initial, very pleasant high of "being in love." But when it actually boiled down to committing to this person in marriage, we *chose* to do it!

In the same way that we choose to love, we can also choose not to allow the difficulties of parenthood to erode our love. When that baby is up all night and you are at your wit's end, instead of kicking your husband, you can gently wake him up and say, "Look, I *really* need your help. I *need* to be held. I *need* your *love*." And when your wife wakes you up, instead of grumbling at her that she is disturbing your sleep and you have to go to work the next day, *hold* her and *love* her. This may not change things. The baby may still wake up several times in the night for a while. Your child will probably get sick with the flu and the chicken pox, and then one day, before you know it, he or she will be taller than you and walk out of your home to make his or her own way in the world. . . The precious years we have to be with our children go by so fast—but so do those years that we have to be with our spouse. So in the still of the night, when you are holding each other, be lovers in the midst of the struggle that is part of life.

Points to Remember

1. Don't blame each other or the children when a problem arises. Blame the situation. Work together to try to solve it.

2. Be a team. Find ways to stay connected through affectionate words, love notes or via lots of hugs, epecially during stressful times.

3. Don't give up finding ways to date each other. If you have to cancel going out on a Friday night due to your child's flu, make another date. Often, much of the stress you are feeling can be relieved just by going out and having fun with each other.

5
Climax Interruptus

How to Cope with Interruptions in Flights of Fancy

If you have ever been embarrassed or interrupted by your children during sex, or even when you are hugging, kissing or trying to talk to each other, you are not alone. If you haven't, then be prepared to have the little buggers scream at the top of their lungs just as you are ready to make beautiful music together, or creep in on you so quietly that you don't even hear them until they ask: "What's that bump in the middle of the bed?"

Little did most of us realize when we decided to have children we would be raising miniature private eyes. They seem to know the precise moment to break up an embrace, or make kissing your spouse seem like the slime of the century: "Oh, you're kissing Mommy! Ooh, dog lips!" If you have not developed a sense of humor, now is the time to do it, along with a few rules of the house. For example, talk to your children about the concept of privacy, and about what type of talk is private within the family and should not be discussed with friends, neighbors or strangers. One mother and father who had prided themselves on being open and honest with their children in discussing the proper names of the genitals, were shocked when their three-year-old son pointed at the waiter in the restaurant where they were eating and asked: "Does he have a penis?" Along with questions like these, if you don't want to hear comparisons of your own anatomy, or what you do when the door is closed, aired in public, you will need to help your children realize what type of talk should remain within your home.

> *"Parenthood: That state of being better chaperoned than you were before marriage."* [1]
> —Marcelene Cox, free-lance columnist

At the moment, let us concentrate on humor, because as one mother said, "If you don't laugh, you'll cry." It is a Saturday morning. You and your spouse have put your four-year-old son in front of a video movie, and made him a cute little tray of orange juice and pancakes with a happy face on them, and slipped away to the bedroom. You lock the door, put some music on and get ready for some heavy duty lovemaking, which you have put on hold all week. Prior to this, you have thoroughly briefed your child by telling him that Mommy and Daddy want to be in their own room to hug and kiss a bit.

Ten minutes later, however, Dorothy and Toto in *The Wizard of Oz* don't seem quite as interesting as what Mommy and Daddy are doing in the bedroom. He comes to the door and begins knocking. Don't get discouraged. You can tell him in a pleasant voice that Mommy and Daddy will be out in a few minutes; then try to take comfort in the fact that this is a learning process for the child.

Gradually, after about two thousand repetitions of your little speech, he will begin to understand Mom and Dad's need for privacy. "When my son began knocking on the door I just started laughing and told my husband Ben, 'Let's pretend it is the hotel manager coming to throw us out, our time is up,'" recalls Shari. Humor is absolutely necessary in the day-to-day interruptions you will inevitably encounter.

It is terribly frustrating to be trying to have a few moments alone to make love, and have your background music be the banging of the door. "Banging to Make Love By," instead of "Music to Make Love By," is not what most couples have in mind. If you tell your son you will be out in a few minutes, he will probably continue to bang on the

A LOVE STORY, FROM A CHILD'S POINT OF VIEW

One summer afternoon, Bob and Joanne were making love during their daughter's naptime. The air was warm and humid so they left the front door open and the screen door locked to let in a little breeze. At last, they had some time to themselves to love and laugh and enjoy every minute of being inside each other. Suddenly, there was a knock on the front door. As they lay in shocked silence, they heard the patter of little feet. It was their three-year-old daughter, Susie, going to the door. Then they heard her say to the person on the other side of the screen door: "My mommy and daddy can't come right now. They are in bed, giggling."

"There was this frantic search for our clothes and the whole time we kept wondering who was at the door, a minister?" recalled Joanne. "I would love to have seen the face of the person on the other side of the screen. It turned out to be a friend of ours, so it was all right. As parents, we get so uptight about things like this, but with kids, it seems to be easier for them."

door and scream for your attention as he does when you are trying to go to the bathroom. If you get dressed and go to the door and tell him you will be out soon, that may only aggravate him more, and cause him to scream louder. While I don't advocate leaving small children unattended for long periods of time, by not going to the door and enjoying a quick ten-minute sexual interlude, you teach your child that Mom and Dad have a right to some private time. If the desire for sex is strong, having quick sex can be better than no sex for you, and more likely to happen. It is possible to have a younger child play in his crib or playpen for ten minutes. For older children, you can put a sign on the door: "Mom and Dad Are Having Fifteen Minutes of Private Time."

Quick sex can be very enjoyable and leave you both feeling closer for several hours afterward. Unfortunately, quick sex has gotten a bad rap. Spouses, more often the wives, feel used, and that this type of sex is bad or cheap. The woman may feel that if she doesn't have an orgasm that sex wasn't so great. The man may complain that it takes over an hour to get his wife aroused enough to have an orgasm. As a result, they allow wonderful opportunities for sex to pass by, and then wonder why they feel frustrated and angry at each other.

MAKE QUICK SEX FUN!

♥ Get the notion out of your head that you both have to experience intense pleasure at the same time. In any good relationship, there is a lot of give and take. One morning you might engage in quick sex to give your husband pleasure. On another morning, you may get the urge for quick sex, and your husband can please you.

♥ Use a lubricant if your husband wants sex and you are not ready.

♥ You can train your mind and body to respond faster if you would like to have an orgasm, says Dr. Ruth K. Westheimer. The trick, she explains, ". . . is to make yourself feel aroused before you actually have sex." [2] You can also prepare yourselves for quick sex by fantasizing, perhaps about the lovemaking you and your husband recently had.

♥ Resist running to your child if he or she is banging on the door, unless it is an emergency. Try to refrain from giving up those precious ten minutes with your husband. Enjoy the little time that you have.

♥ Keep in mind that whatever gives you both pleasure, although not necessarily at the same time, and is not hurtful, brings you both closer and is good. If quick sex also puts you in a good mood, and helps to make you feel less grumpy at each other and the kids, then those ten or fifteen minutes just might be worth it.

HIDING THE GOODS, SO THE KIDS DON'T GET THE GOODS ON YOU

Sometimes, after making love, parents forget to get rid of all the evidence, or return things to the way they were, and *boy*, do they hear about it! If you are caught with incriminating evidence—left your vibrator in the bed, for example—try to stay calm and act nonchalant. Don't toss it around and try to pretend it is a flashlight or an "ear cleaner," as one mother referred to it in the 1989 movie, *Parenthood*. If you feel brave enough, simply tell them it is a vibrator, something Mommy and Daddy use as part of the way they love each other. By being open and remaining calm, you will help your children realize that making love is a natural thing moms and dads do because they are lovers.

"One summer night, after making love, I didn't bother to put my nightgown back on because it was so warm in the house," recalls Lorraine. "In the morning, my two daughters came into our room to greet us as they usually do before going downstairs to watch television. I was naked and Rebecca, my three-and-a-half-year-old got into bed with me. She gasped, immediately turned to me and said, '*Mommy*, you're *naked!*' I told her: 'I was hot!' Rebecca said, 'OK,' but my seven-year-old looked at me with a sly grin and said, 'Oh, *yeah?*'"

Lorraine and her husband Dan refrained from acting like criminals and received the "Golden Lover" award for standing their ground as parents and lovers. "We try to make privacy a positive thing. When our girls are in the bathroom we teach them to say, 'I want my privacy,' instead of saying, 'Get out! I don't want you here.' By saying 'I want privacy,' you are exerting your right to have private time. We are basically building an attitude for them—that we all have a need and right to privacy."

With kids in the house, it is inevitable that at some point they may discover your diaphragm, your rubbers or your lubricating jelly. This is all part of our normal sexual curiosity as human beings. Rather than making your children feel as if they have done something terribly wrong, which may hurt their sexual self-esteem and curtail their curiosity, look at their discovery as an opportunity to talk about sex. Children need to know the truth about the mechanics of sex and about sexually transmitted diseases, particularly about AIDS. They also need to know that the best form of sex is lovemaking within a relationship where there is mutual respect, caring and commitment, such as marriage.

CREATE YOUR PRIVATE SPACE

In teaching our children that we are lovers, we must first impress upon them the fact that a closed or locked door does not mean "come in." Next, we need to create our own space by reclaiming our bedroom. If your bedroom has become the laundry room, a dog kennel, a computer heaven or fast-food chain, now is the time to decorate and make your room *your* room!

In dealing with the locked door issue, you can begin teaching your children at around age two-and-a-half that sometimes parents need time alone together. You can tell your children that if the door is shut, they should knock and that you will do the same for them if their door is shut. For older children who can read, some parents put a sign on the door: "Parents Having Private Time." One couple I spoke to, who have a ten-year-old daughter, said they put this sign on their door: "Body Work in Progress." This is a little too explicit, but you get the idea.

If parents continue to impress upon their children the respect-for-privacy issue, and respect their children's privacy, the kids will learn. One father took his two young boys aside and had a father-son talk with them. By taking the time with his sons to explain the situation, they realized it was a pretty important issue.

"Because we always leave our bedroom door part-way open, when it is shut, the kids know to knock," says Holly, mother of a boy, twelve, and a girl, fifteen. "We taught them to have respect for our privacy at an early age and they have never crossed those lines."

If your child should happen to walk in on you while you and your husband are making love, deal with the interruption calmly and don't make a big deal out of it. If you act like the interruption is a catastrophic event, your child may become frightened and confused.

In addition to instilling the respect-for-privacy notion, parents also need to impress upon children that their bedroom is *their* bedroom, not a place to park dirty sneakers or talk to their friends on the telephone. It is your place to be intimate and you must design that space for the two of you. I'm not saying you have to install a vibrating bed or mirrors on the ceiling, but for starters, candles or soft, full-spectrum lighting, rather than artificial incandescent lighting, can help create a sense of relaxation. If you are lucky enough to possess a cozy fireplace in your bedroom and haven't used it in ages, clean it out and "light that fire"! You will find it will be worth the effort.

Being able to relax and to have a place in your home that is relaxing is *vital*. Some couples I know, particularly moms, often have a difficult time getting in the mood for sex. They fear being interrupted by their children, and feel that there is no place they can go to get away from all the family chaos. Getting rid of various distractions should be number one on your priority list of creating your space. After you have done this, you can then concentrate on creating a sensual environment. For example, your television can be a dis-

---

RECLAIM YOUR BEDROOM FOR SEX!

♥ Put the laundry back where it belongs, in the laundry room. Get those kids, cats and dogs out of your bed! Stale crackers don't belong there, either, so move them out, along with the kids' dirty sneakers, their toys and anything else that creates more of a mood to move to Timbuktu than have sex!

♥ Insist that your children not jump on your bed if they are younger or use your telephone if they are older. This is not their play room. It is *your* play room!

♥ Get rid of any unnecessary furnishings. If you have currently turned your bedroom into your office, gymnasium, library or portrait studio, see if there is another more suitable place for this kind of arrangement. I have yet to interview a couple who can work at their computer and make love at the same time!

---

traction or sexual mood enhancer. If you always watch cop shows or baseball or football games, then get it out of your bedroom. If you have a VCR, then use it to watch romantic movies or soft music videos. Install a stereo or, if there is no room in the budget at the moment to buy one, use a tape recorder to play some romantic mood music you both enjoy.

In fact, if you haven't listened to soft music while making love for a long time, or if you have never done this, now would be a great opportunity to discuss your tastes in music and buy some tapes together. If you are having trouble deciding on some tapes, think back to the music you enjoyed together when you were dating, or on your honeymoon. One couple I know bought a disc that just plays the sound of waves rolling on the beach because it reminds them of their honeymoon in Hawaii. "Music can be important in any sexual expression," relates Kenneth Ray Stubbs, Ph.D., a sexologist who specializes in Sensate Therapy. "It adds an ambiance, along with special scents, candlelight, the warmth or coolness of the room." Soft, new-age music seems to offer the most for enhancing a sexual mood suggests Dr. Stubbs. Tapes, records and discs can be found at any well-stocked record store.

PASSIONATE MUSIC SUGGESTIONS FOR LOVERS

♥ "Down to the Moon," by Andreas Vollenweider

♥ "Silk Road II" and "Ten-Jiku," by Kitaro

♥ "Solo Flight," by Markus Allen

♥ "Petals," by Markus Allen, Jon Bernoff, Dallas Smith and Teja Bell

♥ "Textures," by Greg Joy

♥ "Angel Love," by Aeoliah

Along with lighting and pleasant music, as Dr. Stubbs related, sometimes the air itself can either enhance or inhibit sexual desire. In the winter, the air can get so dry within the home that you feel like your face is going to crack. A good humidifier in your bedroom will minimize this situation and help your body to feel more fluid, less dry and stiff. Opening a window an inch or two, if it is not bitter cold, can make the room feel fresher, less stuffy. In the summertime, an air conditioner always helps if you live in an area of the country that gets especially hot and humid. If you don't have an air conditioner, a fan, of course, will make you feel less sweaty. You can also jump into a cool shower with your spouse, and take turns giving each other body rubs with talcum powder. After all, why should babies have all the fun?

SQUEAKY BED SPRINGS
AND OTHER IRRITATING THINGS

Next, you might want to consider your bed. If yours has been used as a trampoline and is not firm, roomy and quiet you may want to invest in a new one. When my husband and I were living in our apartment in New York City, we could always tell when the couple above us made love. Their bed squeaked loudly and the springs always banged on the floor. If you have a bed like this, and find that sex doesn't have quite the appeal it used to, the reason may be that love moans and groans don't quite go together with squeaky beds. It is like trying to carry on a meaningful conversation with someone, while someone else is running his fingernails over a chalkboard.

While on the subject of beds, I do want to bring up a sensitive problem that has caused a lot of anger and resentment between spouses, but one that can be solved. Several couples I interviewed complained that they just cannot sleep in the same bed with their spouse. Either the wife is a light sleeper and the husband snores, the wife pulls off all the covers or the husband tosses and turns too much. One wife I spoke to was extremely angry at her husband because he kicked her out of bed several times in the night in his sleep. She spent half her night trying to find a comfortable place to sleep—anywhere but with her husband. She was so exhausted and angry that sex with her husband was nonexistent. If you are in a situation like this, consider buying twin beds when you are able to, or two double beds if you have the space. Just because you are married does not mean you have to sleep in the same bed. If sleeping together is causing you to get no sleep and no sex, consider separate beds. Then when you are rested and in the mood for sex, you can always ask: Your bed or mine?

Bedding, in mutually agreeable colors, is also important. Since this is a room for both of you, decisions regarding types of sheets and colors should be something you decide on together. Some people prefer satin sheets, although they are not as sexually enhancing as they appear, because they are so slippery. You may want to go for cotton or flannel sheets, something that will give you some traction.

Sexually appealing smells in your room can also be very sensual, but again, you should choose scents together. Certain scented candles that may be a turn-on for you, may be a turn-off for your spouse. Most importantly, be brave. Choose and use whatever scents, sheets, music and lights you like. Don't be intimidated by your children when they say: "Ooh, what's that icky smell?" Or, "Why do you have all these candles in here? Is it somebody's birthday?" Just tell them very plainly that you are celebrating your love for each other. In fact, the two of you may want to sit down and have a discussion first, to decide on how to explain to your children your lover status. You can show your children the special place where you make love, which is to remain private and free from their toys and clothes. You do not have to go into detail about your sex life. Just tell them you are lovers and your bedroom is the special place where you make love, or, where Mommy and Daddy love each other. Far from being sleazy or wrong, you will be giving your children information that is valuable and right.

A TIME TO TALK

"It is almost like a religious ceremony. After dinner, my husband and I take fifteen minutes to sit, drink our coffee and talk. We share our feelings about our day and the kids are not allowed to interrupt us," explains Cheryl, who has a girl, eight, and boy, ten. "If any one of our children interrupts us more than twice, that child automatically goes to his or her room in a timeout. This is a ritual we started several years ago, and the kids have learned not to interrupt us. They know that our moment together is important and that our relationship is extremely valuable."

Again, kids must learn not to interrupt, but parents must take the time to teach them the value of their relationship. Just telling the child: "Go away. Your mother and I are talking," is not going to do the trick. "I explained to my son who was having trouble understanding this idea by analyzing it this way," says Linda, mother of a seven-year-old. "I told him, 'You don't like it when you are reading a story and someone comes into your room and interrupts you. Mom and Dad like to have uninterrupted time, too.'"

It is harder to get this point across to younger children who may not fully understand, but if you are persistent and consistent in your teaching, your patience will pay off. My husband and I were bowled over once when our youngest daughter who was two-and-a-half years old at the time, and was waiting patiently to speak, suddenly said, "Excuse me. It's my turn to talk!" As young as she was, she had learned to have respect for our talk time, at least for that moment.

Sometimes, children may protest intensely and find all sorts of ways to interrupt their parents' conversation, but don't give up on this issue. During the summertime, I often feed my children early, so my husband and I can have dinner together on the upper deck outside our family room. The children have their dessert and watch a movie inside, while we eat our dinner outside. During the course of teaching them respect for our privacy, we were attacked by woolly ghosts, snowmen with ice cream in their hair and clowns with water balloons, but we didn't give up. Anyone posing as something other than part of the audience of a movie gets benched and sent to bed early. They finally got the idea that watching a movie on video was better than getting an early visit from the sandman.

If there is an emergency, of course, your conversation time will have to be cut short so you can go to your children. Ice cream in the

---

ESTABLISH YOUR OWN TALK RITUAL

♥ Pick a time and place that is relaxing for both of you. For example, talk after dinner in the living room, while the children do their homework in their bedrooms. Or, have dinner, put the children to bed, then talk over dessert and coffee after they have gone to sleep. If you are both just too tired to talk in the evenings, plan to get up before the kids do and talk over breakfast.

♥ Be firm about your ritual, and don't allow distractions to interfere. Put your telephone answering machine on, or let the children take messages.

♥ Teach your children that Mommy and Daddy's time is special, and not to interrupt, unless there is an emergency.

---

hair, bickering between siblings and jelly bean fights, however, do not constitute real emergencies. The kids will survive. Resist the urge to play maid, slave or referee, and be lovers for however many minutes you have allowed yourself adult conversation.

If you have an answering machine for the telephone, turn it on and instruct your children not to pick up the telephone. If you do not have an answering machine, instruct your children in proper telephone etiquette. Role play with them so they will know exactly how they should answer the telephone when you do not want to be disturbed. My six-year-old says: "My parents cannot come to the telephone right now. Will you please call back later?" Older children can be taught to say the same thing, but instead of having the person on the other end of the line call back, write down the caller's telephone number.

If your child is a baby, you can certainly teach him or her to stay amused in a playpen so you and your spouse can have a minimum of fifteen minutes of talk time each evening. One friend of mine puts his daughter in her stroller and parks her in front of the television, so he and his wife can have some time to visit. The baby loves all the sights and sounds of television shows and stays perfectly content for a half hour. "There is still this idea floating around that if you let your child watch television in order to get some time with your spouse that you are a horrible parent," says Sam. "But if your kid is content and not running or crawling naked out into the busy street or being bombarded by sugar-coated cereal ads, then go for it!"

The point is, that parents need to connect verbally each day, as well, and children must learn to respect their parents' need for some uninterrupted conversation. This is a parental right, not something we ask our children permission for, or squeeze in when the children are otherwise occupied. You will be teaching your children a valuable lesson in life by letting them know that Mom and Dad are people, too.

HUGS, HUGS AND MORE HUGS

"When I was a child, I was always scared my parents were going to get a divorce because I never saw them hug or kiss each other," says Carolyn, a mother of three sons, eight months, two years and four years. "I lived in fear of the day they would tell me that they were finally splitting up." Carolyn's parents never divorced. They felt it was just not proper to display any affection in front of their children. Other parents I have spoken to relate similar stories and fears about their parents. Some parents tell me that because they seldom saw their own parents showing affection toward each other, that it is very difficult now for them to show much affection toward their own spouse and even toward their own children.

It appears that cultural and social influences still hit strong the message that "good parents do not display affection for each other in front of their children." Somehow, this behavior is bad. I am talking about hugs and gentle kisses, not blatant sex and passionate puckers. For their own sense of security and happiness, children need to see their parents as lovers in a proper physical light. Even though they may make fun of you when they catch you in the kitchen kissing or hugging, inside, they are delighted because it makes them feel that everything is all right in their world and that it is all right to touch and be touched.

Touching is vital, not only for ourselves as lovers, but for our children to help them realize that appropriate touching between sexes is all right, as well as appropriate displays of affection between parents and their children. The expression of caring and affection through touch, leads to physical trust, which is one of the bases of intimacy. Sexually speaking, when we can learn to express our need

HOW TOUCH, OR LACK OF TOUCH, AFFECTS US ALL

In the 1950's, psychologist Harry Harlow proved just how vital touch is for all of us, and how devastating a lack of touch can be, in his classic experiment with rhesus monkeys. He separated infant rhesus monkeys from their natural mothers and put them in a cage with two surrogate mothers. One surrogate was a warm bare-wire tube with a milk bottle attached to it. The other surrogate was an equally warm cylinder covered with terry cloth. Harlow discovered that the baby monkeys clung to the terry-cloth figure even though the bare-wire surrogate had the milk bottle, which provided these monkeys with their only source of food. When they were confronted with a frightening object, they dashed back to the terry-cloth figure, not to the milk-providing one—to seek comfort. Harlow concluded that these monkeys needed the warmth and security of touch as much as, if not more than, food.

for touch and how we need to be touched often, much of the anxiety about sexual problems and perhaps some of the sexual problems themselves, can be greatly minimized. By kissing and hugging and holding hands, we may be helping our children to avoid potential sexual hang-ups in their future.

"We took our daughter to the beach to fly a kite. As she was flying the kite, my wife and I sat on the beach and started necking," related Marshall, whose daughter Hailey is five. "Suddenly, we heard this laughter. We turned our heads and there was Hailey. She was so happy. We always show lots of affection toward each other and give our daughter lots of affection. Much of this spilled over from all the hugs and kisses given in my family when I was growing up. My parents had a great love for each other. At seventy-years-old, they were still holding hands."

By allowing yourselves to kiss and hug freely, your children will learn that showing affection is important. They will also learn the message that one mother pointed out: "When Mom and Dad go make love it is not such a big deal, but a normal, healthy activity that parents occasionally engage in."

When teaching your children that Mommies and Daddies are lovers, parents must also send the message across that when Mom and Dad are hugging and kissing, children do not interfere. The problem is that younger kids know a good thing when they see it, and will often charge for their parents and run interference between them. You must stand your ground when this happens and not let go of your spouse. Inform you child that Mommy and Daddy are having a private hug and you will give him a family hug and kiss in a minute. Children need attention, too, but try not to give into any guilty thoughts, such as the one that says you must give your child attention the second he demands it, even if he throws a royal temper tantrum. You will again be doing your child a favor by sending a firm message that Mommy and Daddy sometimes have private hugs and kisses.

When you are finished hugging each other, pick your child up, hold him or her between the two of you and give each other a big family hug. Encourage siblings to hug each other, too. Talk about the importance of showing love for each other. As children get older, there is a tendency on the part of parents to show less affection toward them, because they either feel uncomfortable, or feel big kids don't need hugs. But everyone needs hugs and kisses.

In addition to showing affection, it is extremely important to let your child know that it is all right to ask for a hug or kiss. You can teach him or her this idea by asking your spouse for a hug or kiss or shoulder rub when you are feeling in need of affection. Make sure your child hears you when you ask. "Our motto is: 'You need twelve hugs a day just to maintain yourself,' " says Sally, the mother of a seventeen-year-old son. "We all hug and kiss and are not afraid to ask for some nurturing when we've had a bad day and really need it. My son is 6'2" and the biggest huggy bear you have ever seen."

In a world that seems to be reaching higher stress levels every day, touch can be extremely helpful in making us better able to cope. It may also help prevent a lack of sexual desire. If we can feel nurtured through touch daily, we can feel more relaxed and sensual. Touch then, does not become simply a "means to an end," i.e., sexual intercourse. It is another very valuable form of communication, for a better sex life overall.

Points to Remember

1. It is inevitable, with children in the home, that at some point they will discover your diaphragm, birth control pills, *Playboy* maga-

zines or lubricating jelly. This is all part of a normal sexual curiosity. Rather than making your children feel that they have done something wrong, which may hurt their sexual self-esteem, use their discoveries as opportunities to talk to them about sex.

2. You have a right to your privacy. When you lock your door, you are not locking your children out; you are locking your privacy in. Teach your children to respect your need for privacy, and let them know that you will respect their need for privacy, too.

3. Children need to see their parents as lovers in a proper physical sense. Appropriate displays of affection, such as a hug or kiss between you and your spouse, are not wrong. Touching is vital, not only for ourselves as lovers, but for our children, to help them realize that appropriate touching between a man and a woman committed to each other in a relationship is all right, as well as appropriate displays of affection between parents and their children. Everyone needs a hug, especially parents.

6

Romance

How to Bring Out the Lover in Your Spouse

It was a brisk, early Saturday evening. A golden autumn sun was falling gently behind houses across the street. Karen and Bob were in their bedroom getting ready to go out to dinner as they always did on the weekend. Their two teen-age sons had dates of their own and had already left to pick them up. It was also Halloween, and in the streets and on the sidewalks mysterious and funny creatures roamed. Both Karen and Bob had answered the door several times to happy shouts of "Trick or Treat!" Just as Bob was fixing his tie, the doorbell rang again. "Honey, will you get it?" he called to Karen, who had gone downstairs. But when he was met with silence, he went to the door himself. "Trick or Treat!" shouted a grown woman, wearing a sequined mask. She quickly opened her rain coat and revealed her stark naked body. Bob nearly fainted from pleasant surprise, but before he had a chance to speak, the woman had torn off her mask. "Happy Halloween, honey!" said Karen, her heart racing. Bob grinned, and felt his hot flushed face relax a bit. He grabbed Karen, gave her a passionate kiss and whisked her inside the house. Eventually he fixed his tie, but it was close to ten o' clock in the evening before Karen and Bob went out to dinner.

In reading this story, how did it make you feel? Envious? Admit it. Who among us parents would not want to be swept off our feet and fall head-over-heels in love again? "That kind of romance is for adolescents," one mother of a three-year-old son told me. "My husband and I have a more mature love now." In giving me her opinion, however, she did not refrain from mentioning passionate moments she and her husband shared before their son was born.

> *"Today's the day, tonight's the night,*
> *We've shot the stork—so you're all right!"* [1]
> —author unknown

You *can* have passion in your love life again if you stop denying your desire for it, and realize that you *can* create it! Just because you are a parent does not mean you have to give up being a little wild and crazy sometimes. This does not mean you relinquish your responsibilities to your children. But you can allow yourself to let loose once in a while. Dare to take some risks to show your spouse how much you really care. When we become parents there is this underlying notion that we have to be these serious, responsible, no-nonsense people who must put aside all thoughts of passion and romance. But what human being does not want to be pleasantly surprised sometimes, and appreciated? This is what romance is all about!

> *"We are—virtually all of us—in love with love. We crave the exhilaration of wooing and of being wooed; we savor the exalting suspense of courtship. Romance, on the scale of human needs, may not rank quite as high as food or shelter; but it does not fall much farther down. It's one of the things we live for."* [2]
> —Laurence Shames, in his *McCall's* article: "What Men Find Romantic (That Might Surprise You)"

You can begin to create your own romance by setting the right mood. And you can set the right mood by initially letting your spouse know how much you appreciate him or her. Get in the habit of complimenting your spouse often, and saying thank you. A simple: "Thank you for making such a delicious dinner," or "You look so handsome in that suit," will go a long way toward stimulating good feelings between the two of you. One mother told me that she had saved money from her job for months, so she could really give her husband a nice surprise present for his fortieth birthday and show him how much she appreciated him. Lisa made her plans and arranged for a baby sitter for their two sons. Then, one day, in the middle of February, at the time her husband usually comes home from work, he discovered little presents going up the short walk to his front door. Sam opened the first one and it was a slinky bathing suit. He opened the second one, which was a pair of sunglasses, and he opened the third one, which was suntan lotion. When he opened his front door, he was greeted by a big kiss from his wife, and airline tickets to Hawaii! This couple is not wealthy or extravagant. This lucky husband has a wife with a great big heart full of love and appreciation for him. And he, of course, thinks she is the best person in the whole world, and often comes up with ways to show his appreciation for her, such as doing all the grocery shopping and surprising her with special dinners.

> *"I now perceive one immense omission in my* Psychology— *the deepest principle of human nature is the craving to be appreciated."* [3]
>
> —William James, psychologist

The bottom line is that we all want to be put on a pedestal sometimes and told how wonderful we are. This can be sexually exciting! When spouses don't feel appreciated at home, they may begin to look for that appreciation outside the home in the form of extramarital affairs, deny their need for affection and admiration by burying themselves in their work or over-commit themselves to their children.

In addition to complimenting and thanking one another often, we must also *nurture* one another. So often we put so much of our energies into nurturing our children that we forget to nurture our spouse. We mistakenly think that the children can't take care of themselves but that the marriage can.

In finding ways to nurture one another, it is helpful if you can tune into each other's unique needs and desires. A good way to hone in on your spouse's desires and find realistic ways to nurture each other is to fantasize. You might ask your spouse: "If you had your own private butler to take care of you, what would you ask him to do?" Or, you could each make a list of items on separate pieces of paper: "Ways I would like to be nurtured." When you have completed your lists, then exchange and discuss them. You not only create a way to make your wishes known, but most likely you will learn something new about each other.

CREATING ROMANCE

I believe what parents truly desire is a little zip in their relationship now and then, particularly during those difficult times when things may not be going so well and they may be tempted to blame each other. How do we get that zest, that spark, that romance? The key is the element of surprise.

For example, my husband frequently makes long, cross-country business trips to New York City, which are often tiring. We hate to say good-bye and always miss each other. During one particular trip I was wondering how I could somehow touch him so far away. Suddenly, an idea struck. I knew he was due to arrive at his hotel room around one o'clock in the morning. I called the concierge at the hotel and made my arrangements. When my husband walked into his room, the first thing he saw was a nice bottle of wine, a fruit and cheese plate, and my love note, which said I had hoped he had a nice flight and how much I cared. He was deeply touched, and not about to be outdone.

The next day, I received an airline ticket in the mail and a love note asking me to spend the weekend with him in New York. My heart began soaring as I thought of the possibilities. My brain kept bringing me down to earth: "You've never been that far away from your children. How are you going to get a baby sitter on such short notice? What if there is an emergency? How could you spend that much money on something so frivolous?"

I was not to be deterred, and let my heart do the talking. I managed to get a baby sitter my children have known for two years and in whom I felt a lot of confidence. And I said the money is an investment in my marriage, and ultimately in my family—and took off. The intense excitement my husband and I managed to generate from pulling off our tryst was just as thrilling, if not more so, than the "high" we felt when we first fell in love!

LOVING WAYS TO NURTURE YOUR SPOUSE

♥ Surprise your spouse with a hot cup of coffee when he or she emerges from a morning shower.

♥ Put some fresh flowers in a vase and place it near the bathroom sink or on your spouse's dresser. Men like to get flowers just as much as women.

♥ Lay out your spouse's night clothes on the bed, just like valets do on cruise ships and fancy hotels.

♥ Put a love note, with a mint, on your spouse's pillow, and tell the kids to keep their hands off!

♥ Take turns washing each other's hair, preferably while in the shower together.

♥ Fix each other a nice fruit and cheese plate and a glass of wine at the end of a hectic day.

♥ Take turns putting the kids to bed if one of you has had an especially tiring day. For example, if your wife has had some dental work done, and is just not up to putting any child to bed, then take over for her. And don't forget to make her a cup of tea. And if your husband has to work late, and you know he is going to be exhausted, try to get the kids ready for bed, or in bed, *before* he comes home.

♥ Run a bath for your spouse, and don't forget the bubbles. Men don't like to admit it, but they would like to have a few bubbles.

♥ Go ahead and fill up the car with gas if your spouse is always forgetting and runs it to empty. Instead of yelling at him or her, take care of this job as a favor to your spouse. One woman I interviewed, whose husband always filled up her car for her, thought this gesture was more romantic than receiving flowers.

♥ Give each other a short break at the end of a busy day, and protect each other's time. For example, if your husband is resting for ten minutes, do not allow the children to bother him, and take down a message if someone calls on the telephone. And husbands, do the same for your wives.

> *"When you have to devise something new, something that will*
> *really surprise your partner... you have to begin to think*
> *about yourself and who you are, as well as what is expected*
> *from you. Then you have to come up with something that will*
> *change you in some way—which, in turn, necessitates a*
> *change in your partner in response to your innovation."* [4]
> —Dr. Fred Gottlieb, a psychiatrist and director
>   of the Family Therapy Institute of Southern
>   California

Change shakes up your relationship and can stimulate some exciting emotional sparks that can turn you on to each other. In fact, researchers now know that while too much stress can turn you off to each other, a little stress and anxiety created by something like a pleasant surprise, can turn you on.

> *"The flow of adrenaline triggered by stress creates a physical*
> *tension that, in the right amounts, your body can translate*
> *into sexual arousal."* [5]
> —David H. Barlow, Ph.D., director of the Center for
>   Stress and Anxiety Disorders, and professor of
>   psychiatry at SUNY, Albany

A good example of this is what happened to a friend of mine one night. She was downstairs in her laundry room folding clothes and received a telephone call at ten o'clock in the evening. "I couldn't imagine who would be calling so late," remembers Shirley. "Then I heard this mysterious-sounding voice say: 'Would you like to make love?' I was *shocked*, then I suddenly realized it was my husband Dan, calling me on the bedroom telephone! I stammered: 'I'll be up in two seconds!'" This really added a nice spark to Shirley and Dan's relationship. He still calls her on the telephone, but she never knows when, and that is the surprise, the excitement!

The surprise can be anything, as long as it is unpredictable: a totally new hairdo, a sexy dress when you normally never wear sexy clothes or some exotic foods you have never tried before. One man totally shocked his wife by throwing her a surprise birthday party, but not just any party. It was a child's surprise party, something his wife secretly always wanted because she never had one as a kid. Her

---

ENTICING WAYS TO SET THE SCENE FOR ROMANCE

♥ Leave little mysterious hints around the house in the form of love notes, where only your spouse would see them: "See you at ten o'clock in the boudoir. You bring the wine; I'll wear my teddy!"

♥ Call each other up on the telephone and fantasize about the evening you are going to have together.

♥ Take the kids to grandma's house, if you are lucky enough to have relatives nearby. *Then* call your husband up and say: "Guess what? It's just you and me tonight!"

♥ Spray one of your scarves with his favorite perfume then casually leave it on the surface where he usually looks at the mail when he comes home.

♥ Don't rush to get out of your street clothes, after the kids are in bed. Take turns slowly undressing each other. . .

---

husband had guests bring kiddie toys, and he had a Cinderella birthday cake made, with a pink sparkling coach and white horses on top. She adored her husband's thoughtful gesture which helped them engage in thoughtful, tender lovemaking later.

Romance is in the heart of the romancer. It is what you and your spouse want it to be. For some couples, it is a candlelit soak in the bathtub. For others, it is a bike ride on a country road, and for still others, it is having dinner in the van, parked in the driveway, after the children go to sleep.

> *"Some things, like moonlight, are romantic by their very nature. Other things, neutral in themselves, become romantic by circumstance, by the part they play in a relationship. And it's those things—the things whose romantic connotations we define for ourselves—that can be the most intimate and resonant of all."* [6]
>
> —Laurence Shames, in his *McCall's* article: "What Men Find Romantic (That Might Surprise You)"

ROMANCE BY CIRCUMSTANCE

- ♥ Go to a drive-in movie because it reminds you of when you first started dating.
- ♥ Share one soda with two straws.
- ♥ Take a hike in the woods.
- ♥ Visit an art gallery to look at the work of your favorite artist.
- ♥ Ride bikes, ice skate or swim in a pool and hug each other in the water.

Creating romance does take work. It doesn't just happen like a bolt of lightening, yet for one reason or another, we begin making excuses once the children come along. I have heard everything from: "The kids take up all of our time and energy," to "Why should I be the one to start the ball rolling?" In order to help parents get over those hurdles they place in front of themselves, I felt it was vital to delve into the many reasons why we seldom initiate passionate gestures and events. Many couples continue to sabotage their desires and impulses, even though they know darn well that sometimes, parents just want to have fun!

HOW TO BEAT THE GUILT TRAP

When Merle, the mother of a ten-year-old son and seven-year-old daughter, turned thirty-five, she and her husband celebrated for two nights in a row with friends on Union Street in San Francisco. They went to a lively nightclub, drank beer, told jokes with the waiters and danced. At one point, Merle got up on stage and did a little jig herself after a bit of brew and prodding from her friends. "We just had a blast!" she recalled. "It was the kind of place I used to go to in college where everyone drank beer, got a little rowdy and had a lot of fun. I didn't want it to be over, but you know, you always pay for it in the end." "What do you mean?" I asked her. "Well, you end up feeling guilty because you had so much fun away from the kids," she replied.

STOP FEELING GUILTY!

♥ Remind yourself that your needs are important, too.

♥ Remind yourself that in order to maintain a strong relationship, you and your husband need time together just to relax and have fun.

♥ Realize that you are being good role models for your children. You don't want them to grow up to be martyrs, do you? Of course not!

♥ Realize that if you *don't* take time out to have fun and recharge your parental batteries, you will more likely be tired and grouchy and less able to be the patient parent you want to be.

♥ Realize that if your children give you a hassle about going out, it is because they may just be experiencing some separation anxiety. It is not because they don't want you to have fun. Talk to them about where you will be going, and what you will be doing. Allow them to help you get ready by letting them help you put on your shoes, or pick out your jewelry. Small children love doing this, and it enables them to cope better with your leaving.

♥ Refrain from calling home twenty-five times to see how the children are doing. You don't have to do this to prove you are a good parent. You are already being a good parent by being good to yourself.

♥ Don't spend your whole evening talking about the kids. You are not being selfish parents when you take time to talk about yourselves and adult interests.

♥ Remember, when you give yourselves a good time, you are not only building a strong relationship, you are also building a strong family.

Merle, like many parents today, carries around within her this unrealistic sense of parental duty, a burden that can put a damper on a potentially enjoyable evening, or the memory of it. For some couples, it prevents them from going out together, except when they must attend weddings, funerals or PTA meetings. In order to maintain romance and intimacy in your relationship, you and your spouse must make time to date each other. Parents who have established weekly dates tell me that this is truly essential for them to feel connected. You may not always go out, but it is crucial that you set aside one evening a week to do nothing but spend time doing something fun with your spouse.

> *"Planning for intimate times together not only makes these moments more likely to happen, but also lets you look forward to the pleasure you'll share together—whatever that pleasure may be."* [7]
>
> —Lonnie Barbach, Ph.D., psychologist and sex therapist

HELPFUL WAYS TO MAKE LEAVING YOUR KIDS EASIER

♥ Let them know in the morning that you will be going out that night. This way, they can get used to the idea and ask questions when you are more relaxed, and not frantically trying to get ready.

♥ Talk to your child even if he or she is a baby. He or she may not understand what you are saying, but the matter-of-fact tone of your voice will be reassuring.

♥ Never, ever, try to slip out the back door when the baby sitter comes, thinking that if your child does not see you leave, he or she will not be upset. Most likely, your child will be *more* upset. You want to build up a relationship of trust with your child, not feed his or her fears of abandonment by not being honest.

♥ Make the time you are gone a fun time for your children. Allow them to make ice cream sundaes with the baby sitter, and watch a favorite movie.

♥ Let them know about what time you will be coming home. For children under the age of five who have no concept of time, tell them you will be home after they have gone to bed. Assure them that you will check on them when you come home and give them a kiss.

For many parents, allowing themselves to have fun without their children is a "growing away process." If you are new parents, it is all right to allow yourselves time away from your baby gradually and a chance to get used to leaving junior with a baby sitter, so do it! Go out for coffee for two hours close to home at first, then extend the time and distance.

As a parent myself, I understand that it is not easy to separate from the children, especially if one or more of them is screaming his or her lungs out and clinging to you like a leech, while your husband is waiting impatiently for you in the car. Focus on your relationship, and know that you are doing the kids a favor in the long run by spending some intimate time as a couple. If you have managed to find a baby sitter you feel comfortable with, your kids will most likely stop crying within fifteen minutes after you have left the house, and you will return a much calmer, patient parent because you have been nurtured, too.

"It is almost like you have to train yourself to think and say, 'Getting out with my spouse is essential in order for me to be a good parent, a good wife and a good person,' " says Carol, the mother of two teen-age daughters. "A lot of people don't give themselves the chance to say, 'It is all right to have time with my spouse without the children.' I'm sure if it were a requirement of the marriage contract that you go out so many times per month to have fun with your spouse, that people would not resist it and feel they are deserting their kids."

Establish and Maintain Your Baby-Sitter Support System

Going out means leaving your child in the care of a baby sitter, and for many parents this is hard. It is part of the reason they seldom go out, or are reluctant to go out. But the more you do it, the easier it gets. It is also easier to go out if you feel confident in your baby sitter. Finding a baby sitter you feel you can trust takes work, but it is worth it! Ask your pediatrician, minister, rabbi, priest, friends or neighbors for recommendations of baby sitters. You might even call directors of parent support groups and nursery schools. Some nursery schools hire teen-agers to lend a hand with their children after school, and these same responsible teen-agers are also looking for more baby-sitting jobs.

In order to feel confident in the baby sitter you have found, you must orientate her to your children, your schedules and your house. One thing I have discovered is that when you set down rules and let the baby sitter know exactly what is expected of him or her—when you give the baby sitter the information he or she needs regarding your children and your home—everything goes much more smoothly and you are more apt to have and keep a regular baby sitter. You can also enjoy a good time and not feel you have to call home every twenty minutes. It is surprising how few parents fully inform baby sitters, however, and I can understand why. "Sometimes, when you've decided you are going out and have finally found a baby sitter and made all the arrangements, you are anxious just to get out of the house!" one mother of three lively boys told me.

HOW TO HIRE A BABY SITTER—A CHECKLIST

- ♥ Obtain a list of at least five references and call each reference.

- ♥ Find out how long this particular baby sitter sat for these various families; how they felt about this sitter and if there were any problems. Find out why the baby sitter left, if he or she did, or how he or she is doing currently if still baby-sitting for this "reference family."

- ♥ Ask the baby sitter about his or her experience, during the interview and try to get to know the sitter as a person.

- ♥ Remember to ask the baby sitter about his or her driving record; if he or she has had any traffic violations in the past three years.

- ♥ Have the baby sitter spend time interacting with your children and see how he or she does with them. After the sitter has gone, you can even ask your older children what they thought of the baby sitter.

- ♥ Arrange for a trial period, if you like the baby sitter. Plan to be doing things in your home for the first two or three times your baby sitter sits to see how he or she does with your kids, and to be available if he or she has any questions.

HOW TO HELP YOUR BABY SITTER—A CHECKLIST

♥ Help the sitter get acquainted with your children. Tell him or her about each child's personality, likes and dislikes, hobbies, favorite toys and games.

♥ Explain your method of discipline and how you want your baby sitter to handle sibling fights or unacceptable behavior.

♥ Explain your children's bedtime schedules, routines, favorite toys they like to sleep with, and whether or not they sleep with a night light, if you are going out for the evening. Don't forget to give the baby sitter some helpful suggestions for what he or she can do if the children have trouble going to sleep.

♥ Familiarize the baby sitter with your home. Make sure he or she knows how to operate all door locks, so the kids can get out fast if there is an emergency. Tell the baby sitter where the fuse box, first-aid kit, flashlight, candles and matches are kept. Also, give the name and telephone number of a nearby neighbor whom he or she can go to in the event of an emergency. Be sure to show the baby sitter where you keep all important telephone numbers, such as police, fire department and your doctor.

♥ Be sure to write down the address and telephone number of where you can be reached, and explain at what point he or she should call: if there is an emergency only, or, if your child is having difficulty getting to sleep.

♥ Explain your rules of the house. For example, if you do not allow children to have food or drinks in your living room, let the baby sitter know.

♥ Explain other rules regarding baby-sitting. If you don't want the baby sitter having friends over, or talking on your telephone all evening, be sure to explain this rule. You can say in a very matter-of-fact way that you do not allow any friends in your home when baby sitters are watching your children, nor frequent or long telephone conversations.

♥ Let your baby sitter know the time when you plan to be home, but be sure to call if you are going to be much later than this time.

Parents who have not taken the time fully to prepare the baby sitter, however, may come home to a few surprises, and in the end, lose some potentially good baby sitters. "I'll never hire that baby sitter again. She let the kids have cookies on the rug and didn't clean the dishes she used," one mother of two-year-old twins complained.

One father returned from a party, drove the baby sitter home and was outraged when he looked in his freezer to discover she had wiped him out of his favorite chocolate ice cream. The parents had forgotten to go over the do's and don'ts of raiding the refrigerator for snacks.

Still another couple came home nervous wrecks, because every time they tried to call home, their telephone was busy. They had forgotten to set down rules with the baby sitter about the use of the telephone and having friends call.

If your baby sitter is a mature, experienced woman and is a mother herself, she may feel more comfortable in a strange house and realize what needs to be done. If she is a teen-ager, she is going to need specific instructions as to what you want her to do. After all, if she feels uncomfortable because she has been left uninformed, she may not want to baby-sit for you again, and tell you she is busy when you call to hire her.

In setting down rules, remember that your rules may be different from your friends' rules. You will have to design a system that works for you by thoroughly discussing your expectations with your spouse. You may not care if the baby sitter eats all your favorite ice cream, but your husband may, and arguing about it after a wonderful evening out will surely put a damper on any after-date lovemaking possibilities.

Leaving Your Child Home Alone

If your children are nearing age eleven or twelve, and on the verge of being able to stay home by themselves without a baby sitter, you may want to test the waters by taking short trips away from the house during the day. But a word of caution here. Deciding when to leave a child is not always a matter of age. A mature nine-year-old, for example, may be left safely, while an impulsive thirteen-year-old may not. It is a matter of knowing how well your child copes with everyday problems, and how well he or she is able to communicate with you and other people. If an emergency does arise when your

---

HOW TO DESIGN YOUR OWN SET OF RULES

- ♥ Sit down with your spouse when you have a quiet moment after the children are in bed.

- ♥ Talk about what your expectations are regarding baby sitters who watch your children.

- ♥ Discuss which issues are important to you and which issues are not so important. If rules regarding the use of the telephone are something you want to enforce, then write them down. If the snacks your sitter eats are not a big deal, then don't bother.

---

child is alone, he or she may have to call on someone else and must be able to verbalize the situation clearly. Generally, eleven or twelve is a good age to leave a child because "this is the point of development when children have a more rational sense of right and wrong," says Rogelio Hernit, M.D., assistant professor of psychiatry at Penn State's Milton S. Hershey Medical Center in Hershey, Pennsylvania.

Before leaving your child alone, precautions must be taken. Be sure to establish a back-up system, a neighbor your child can turn to in case of an emergency. Also, check to see if you have proper locks and your child knows how to operate them. You may want to install smoke detectors if you don't already have them, and organize practice fire drills. Make sure your child has easy access to emergency telephone numbers. If there are several children in the house, try not to overburden the oldest sibling with too much responsibility, or be gone too frequently or for long periods. One mother who has a twelve-year-old, a ten-year-old and a four-year-old pays the two older children $1.50 an hour for watching the youngest child, putting her to bed and maintaining calm in the house. She pays the four-year-old a penny an hour for as long as she is awake for helping to keep things calm, too.

In order to tell if your child is ready, leave for short periods and see how he or she does. If your child is not able to obey instructions, becomes overly frightened or can't handle little problems that pop up, he or she may not be ready to be left alone just yet. Another word of caution. If your child is having emotional difficulties—as a result of a close relative's death—then he or she should not be left alone. "When children are subjected to traumatic events, they tend to regress and can become frightened," explains Dr. Rogelio Hernit.

How a child handles himself depends a lot on how he or she has been raised. You can do a great deal to help your children cope with being alone by being honest with them. By always telling your children when you are going out, where you are going and when you will return, they will be able to adapt much better than if you try to sneak out the backdoor as soon as the baby sitter arrives. In developing a sense of trust with your child, you will be building his or her capacity for dealing with separations. Your child will become a stronger person, rather than an overly dependent one.

Parents who are finally able to leave their children home alone report an exhilarating sense of freedom. "It's so nice to just be able to

---

ENCOURAGING WAYS TO PREPARE
YOUR CHILD FOR STAYING HOME ALONE

- ♥ Write down the name and telephone number of the place you will be, plus the name and telephone number of at least two neighbors your child can call in an emergency. Leave a house key with one of these neighbors.

- ♥ Let your child know an approximate time of when you will return, and call if you are going to be late.

- ♥ Show your child your list of emergency telephone numbers of the police, fire department and doctor.

- ♥ Go over house rules, such as not opening the door to strangers, and how to answer a telephone caller who asks to speak with you. Your child should be taught to say: "My mother can't come to the telephone right now. Please call back later." Instead of saying: "My mother and father aren't home."

- ♥ Explain house rules to each child if you have more than one child you are leaving home alone. Go over house rules with each of them and tell them where they can reach you or a neighbor.

---

go out and not have to call ten people to see who can baby-sit," one mother told me. If you have arrived at this point, congratulations! You can feel proud that you have prepared your children well. They are giving you a great gift and you have given yourselves a great gift, precious moments to be lovers.

If you are still finding and training sitters, however, don't get discouraged. It is a lot of effort, but that effort is well worth it.

HOW TO BREAK OUT OF THE WEB OF BOREDOM

Not long after the honeymoon is over, and even more so after the kids are born, we fall into this rut of unrealistic expectations. We expect our spouses to read our minds and hearts and to discover what we really want and need. And when they don't, we become bitterly disappointed, resentful and assume that the romance has gone out of the marriage. In addition, we are dealing daily with the tremendous stress that raising children entails, which does not exactly leave much room to be Princess or Prince Charming. Rather than pointing the finger at our situation and trying to find a way to make things better, however, we blame our spouses for letting us down and not fulfilling our dreams. We even may go so far as to begin disliking qualities about each other that attracted us in the first place.

Unfortunately, real life is not a romantic fairy tale and I doubt if many of us would want it to be. The prince and princess marry, and have a baby who spits up and cries a lot. There are bills to be paid and laundry to be done. How can anyone be "Jumpin' Jack Dashing" all the time? The answer is you *can't*, but you *can* start right now to create an environment that would be conducive to romance, and bring out the lover in your lover. We all have faults. No one is perfect. Everyone is incompatible in one way or another.

So stop blaming your spouse for what he or she is or is not; what he or she does or does not do. A happy marriage and sex life is possible. But it takes some courage: being brave enough to admit you are wrong when you are wrong; concentrating on the good qualities of your spouse instead of on his or her faults; telling your spouse what you really want and need; and compromising at times to solve problems and break down the walls that separate the two of you.

One friend of mine felt her marriage was really lacking in the romance department and wanted to spice it up. I asked her, if she could have a perfectly romantic evening, what would it be? "Well, first of all, I would send the children to my mother's house to spend the night, then I would greet my husband at the door wearing something really sexy that I could easily slip out of," began Joyce. "I would offer him a drink and we would sit in front of a cozy fire, tell dirty jokes and laugh ourselves silly. Then we would have a delicious dinner by candlelight and have a stimulating conversation about art or music. Eventually, we would stroll into the bedroom, give each other a massage and make wonderful love."

"That sounds terrific," I told her. "Have you set a date, yet?" "Are you kidding?" she replied. "Ron would think I flipped or something. I'd be afraid he wouldn't notice. I don't know how he would be with me. We've been just 'Mom' and 'Dad' for so long."

It took Joyce several days to get up her courage to tell Ron about her fantasy, but once she did, she was surprised to see how receptive he was. "Ron thinks this is a great idea, and wants to plan it with me," said Joyce. "He thought our love life was getting boring, too, but was afraid to say anything."

Joyce and Ron had a terrific night together, made possible by the fact that they were finally open about their true feelings and desires. It is sad that "fear of intimacy" strikes so many couples so often that any potential for spicing up the relationship gets lost unnecessarily. Even when couples have been married several years and have been through the most vulnerable aspects of childbirth together, there is still this great fear of revealing their innermost thoughts and feelings. "They rarely say exactly what they think and feel, openly and honestly. Instead, they say something entirely different that seems 'safer'. . . and then they wonder why they feel so ineffectual in their dealings with others," says Nathaniel Branden, Ph.D., executive director of the Biocentric Institute, a counseling center in Beverly Hills, California.[8] We sort of give hints about what we really think and feel, hoping our partner will pick up on our thoughts. When he or she doesn't, we then become very frustrated and resentful. Often, this behavior and response is the result of not having adequate role models while growing up. Our own parents perhaps dealt with each other in this manner and we learned it from them. It is also often *difficult* for many of us to express our true feelings because in childhood we either *weren't permitted* to express them, or when we did express our wants and desires they weren't taken very seriously.

Many husbands and wives really want to be emotionally closer, but are *unable* to reach that intimate place. They draw near to each other, then pull away. They manage to reach a certain level of intimacy, but can go *no further* because the *anxiety* this creates becomes too much for them to handle.

Intimacy fears may be painful to face, but it is crucial that you deal with them and try to solve them, not only for the sake of your own marital happiness, but for your children's happiness, as well. You *can* break the chain of non-communication and also help ensure for your children a happy marriage in the future.

Intimacy Island

In her work with many couples to help them get back in touch with each other, Dr. Debora Phillips, a behavior therapist in Beverly Hills and author of *How to Give Your Child a Great Self-Image* (Random House, 1989), has designed a technique, which has proven to be successful with many husbands and wives. She calls it "Intimacy Island," a method couples can spend as few as ten minutes a day on, although twenty minutes is better. This method not only helps couples to communicate better with each other, but also helps to dispel tension. "Two people sit down together and do some form of relaxation for a minute or two," says Dr. Phillips. "They can do this by using imagery, by imagining that they are at the ocean or in the mountains, for example.

"First, each person takes a turn giving the other person a compliment. The person receiving the compliment needs to say thank you, not discount the compliment, not try to get away from it, but just say thank you and make eye contact. This is a way of beginning on a positive note.

"The second thing I have couples do is each person takes a turn asking a discovery question. The idea is to try to find out something new. It can relate to the person's taste in music, food, clothes, places of travel, anything. This is a way for couples to further remove themselves from everyday problems onto an intimacy island.

"The third step is to take turns expressing a vulnerabilty. It can be a fear, a hope, a doubt—something that you wouldn't want the world to know, but that you can trust this person with. The important part of this step is not so much the information the person is expressing as much as the ability of the other person to be empathetic. The person acting as the listener should not give advice, discount what the person is saying or try to solve the problem. He or she should merely listen with empathy, to try to get inside the other person's skin. The listener can say: 'I know that can be difficult to feel that way,' or 'I understand why this is upsetting you.' He or she should *not* say: 'Oh, if you had only planned your day better you wouldn't be so tired.'

"Lastly, each person either takes a turn talking about one characteristic he or she likes about himself or herself, or talking about one characteristic he or she would like to change."

In communicating with your spouse and creating a romantic environment, you have to be willing to risk being vulnerable and realize that your spouse has fears, too. At the same time, you also have to be an attentive listener. Try to empathize, not judge. Listen to your spouse's feelings behind the words.

Many couples who have opened up with each other, who have learned to talk and have fun, report that they enjoy a more frequent and spontaneous sex life.

HOW TO KEEP COURTING YOUR LOVER

After couples get married, and especially after the children appear on the scene, spouses get this notion that the hunt is over. They no longer have to try to look sexually appealing to win their spouse. They fall into a routine of just not trying anymore, using the excuse that they have no time to pay specific attention to themselves. With kids to take care of, jobs to go to, a house to run, they say they are just trying to survive. At the same time they stop trying to make themselves more interesting and appealing, they also stop exploring their mate—asking his or her opinion daily about art, literature, sports, specific current events, dreams or goals.

If you think you already know everything about your spouse, then ask your mate these questions sometime. His or her answers may surprise you. If you won a million dollars, what would you do with the money? If you could choose to live anywhere in the world for two years, where would you live and why? How would you spend your last day on earth?

QUESTIONS TO EXPLORE WITH YOUR SPOUSE

In his marvelous book, *The Book of Questions*, author Gregory Stock, Ph.D., poses over two hundred questions that couples and friends can explore together so they can find out more about each other. "Too frequently we pull back from bringing up questions that seem awkward or intrusive, yet these are the very ones that will open paths to understanding and intimacy," says Dr. Stock.[9] Here are some exciting questions from his book:

♥ If you were able to live to the age of ninety and retain either the body or the mind of a thirty-year-old for the last sixty years of your life, which would you want?

♥ Whom do you admire the most? In what way does this person inspire you?

♥ If you could wake up tomorrow having gained any one ability or quality, what would it be?

♥ Are there people you envy enough to want to trade lives with them? Who are they?

♥ What is your most treasured memory?

♥ If you went to a dinner party and were offered a dish you had never tried, would you want to taste it even if it sounded strange and not very appealing?

♥ If you could have free, unlimited service for five years from an extremely good cook, chauffeur, housekeeper, masseuse or personal secretary, which would you choose?

♥ Does the fact that you have never done something increase or decrease its appeal to you?

♥ If you went to a beach and it turned out to be a nude beach, would you stay and go swimming? Would you swim nude?

♥ What do you like best about your life? Least?

Human beings are endlessly complex. We are each a self-contained adventure—with dreams, thoughts and feelings to explore. If your sex life or life in general has become routine and boring, consider courting each other again. *Take time to make yourself and your partner feel special.* In fact, if you want to keep the excitement going in your relationship, marriage counselors advise couples to treat each other as if they are always in courtship. This lost art involves always trying to look attractive and be interesting for yourself and your spouse, thinking up thoughtful gestures, saying "I love you" often and just plain having fun.

Keeping Up Appearances

"I never assume that I've caught my man," relates the mother of five children, ranging in age from eight to twenty. "There are so many temptations that I never let go of my efforts to be appealing for my husband."

"Keep up your physical appearance as much as possible," urges a mother of a teen-ager, happily married for twenty-five years. "Maybe you will have to make a dress, instead of buy one, but be creative in trying to initiate that special touch."

Smart wives, like these women, make sure their hair is always neatly groomed. They wear makeup and get their nails manicured, or do their nails themselves. They wear clothes that flatter their bodies. And they wear perfume. They do whatever makes them feel good about themselves, and know it will make their husbands feel good looking at them.

Smart husbands, too, make efforts to keep themselves looking good. They shave and take care of their fingernails. They might wear cologne and make sure their hair is clean and well-groomed.

One woman who was feeling overweight and unattractive after her second child was born, bought black lacy underwear, which she wore on a date with her husband. "As we sat down at the dinner table I whispered to him, 'Oh, by the way, you should see the new undies I have on,' " related Sharon. "They really made me feel sexy and started our whole evening off on a sexy note."

For Darlene and her husband Jim, married twenty-four years and the parents of four children, taking baths and making the effort to look nice for each other is a ritual they have established in preparing for their Saturday night date. "It's sort of a cleansing process, and

---

LOOK AND FEEL SEXY

♥ Wear perfume or cologne if it is something you like to do.

♥ Arrange time in your busy schedule to do your own nails or get a professional manicure.

♥ Concentrate on wearing clothes that will flatter your shape, no matter what shape you have.

♥ Change shampoo brands once in a while and experiment with stylish barrettes.

♥ Dare to be daring sometimes. Wear black or red lacy underwear. Buy your spouse some sexy underwear, too.

---

there's something in that process that makes you really look forward to going out—whether it's just for a long walk or to dinner somewhere," says Darlene. "It's nice to know that my husband has a smooth chin because he wants to please me, and he appreciates it when I wear perfume."

Looking good for each other makes you want to be closer emotionally and physically. This is how you caught each other's interest in the first place. It is also a good way to keep each other interested.

Counting the Ways

Gestures of love also go a long way to adding a feeling of courtship. These gestures can be serious, silly or sexy. Courting, after all, should be fun.

"Sex doesn't always have to be an expression of endless, abiding love and passion. It can be mindless or naughty or funny." [10]
—Dagmar O'Connor, director of the Sex Therapy Program at St Luke's-Roosevelt Hospital Center, New York

"I sent my husband this sexy card once that looked like the blueprint of a golf course, but when you looked closer, it was actually an outline of the penis inside the vagina," related Sandy, mother of a five-year-old son. "I wrote some note on the inside about wanting to be with him that night. Another time, after we recently bought our house that had a backyard full of weeds, I sent him this card that showed a couple in bed hugging and kissing, and outside the bedroom window was this beautiful garden full of flowers."

One father told me that he calls his wife several times a day to tell her he loves her. "It's a nice habit to get into, and makes us feel connected even when we are apart," he says.

Another father travels around town a lot in his job, but whenever he is near his home at lunchtime, he stops by to visit with his wife. It's a great time for an afternoon delight, they told me, because the kids are in school.

Still another couple I interviewed, married twenty-seven years with two older sons, told me that whenever they go out, they always order one dessert with two forks. "We started out in our marriage not having much money, so whatever we were able to do we had to do simply, and sharing like this has made us feel closer over the years," says Jack. His wife Helen agrees: "It just became a romantic thing to do."

Peter, the father of two daughters, six and eight years, told me he and his wife have fun even doing seemingly mundane things and often think about their very first date. "Cheryl says she will always remember it because I asked her if she wanted to go have ice cream, instead of going to a bar for a drink. She thought this was a cute idea and liked doing that so much better. It's just the little things that count when you enjoy being with someone."

Whether you share a dessert or spend ten minutes writing a love note, gestures like these count a great deal in a relationship. And the fun part is that the ideas you can come up with are endless.

A Toast to You!

In going out together, which is crucial, there are dates, and then there are *dates*. If you go out together and then spend the whole evening discussing the kids and problems at home or with work, you are not going to have a very good time and be less inclined to go on dates. Often, there is a great need to talk about what is going on with the kids, the house and the jobs, because for most busy parents this is the only time they have to be alone.

AFFECTIONATE GESTURES THAT HELP KEEP LOVE ALIVE

♥ Call each other on the telephone and say "I Love You."

♥ Compliment each other frequently.

♥ Say "thank you" when your spouse has cooked a good dinner, made that extra effort to pick up your shirts at the cleaners or remembered to get the milk at the store that you needed.

♥ Send sexy or silly cards, or place them somewhere in the house where only your spouse will see them.

♥ Try to tune into what your spouse would really like, when you buy presents. Buy her lacy panties instead of a blender for Mother's Day. Buy him a sexy sweater instead of a drill for Father's Day.

♥ Kidnap your spouse and take him or her on a surprise date.

♥ Trade baby-sitting services with your neighbor or have your mother take the kids for a night so you can have fun with your spouse in your own home.

♥ Have an indoor picnic. If you have a chance to be home alone, cook up an exotic meal, something different, and eat somewhere other than in your kitchen or dining room.

♥ Try to look nice for yourself and your spouse. It will make you both feel good about yourselves and each other.

♥ Tune into to the world around you and try to learn something new or interesting each day to talk to your spouse about. Read the newspaper for ten minutes or listen to the news while driving in your car.

♥ Ask each other's opinion on current events or about a fascinating fact.

♥ Ask questions about each other's hopes, goals and dreams, and be an empathetic listener. When you tune into what your spouse is feeling and thinking, you strengthen your bonds of intimacy.

♥ Make plans for a romantic weekend away, whether it be at a cozy mountain cabin or seaside resort. Surprise your spouse with a handmade invitation and a bottle of his or her favorite wine. Time alone will give you the opportunity to focus on each other and leave the pressures and distractions of home life behind for a weekend.

Couples I have interviewed that have fun on their dates, relate that they always limit the time they discuss family issues. Some parents get their family or work topics out of the way first, by talking in the car before they get to the restaurant. Other parents discuss family concerns between the time they order their meal and before the first course is served. Once the appetizers come, there is no more talk about the kids, the house, the job, the car or the dog. Couples bent on having fun, talk about current events, wine, food, music, art, literature, camping, vacations, good times they have had in the past and even sex.

"A lot of times we talk about when we were dating before we married and some of the risks we've taken, like going rafting down a river and making love on the river bank," recalled Julie, mother of two boys, nine months and two years. "That kind of reminiscing gets us set up for an exciting evening."

Another couple enjoys keeping each other up on current events. "I tell a lot of my friends who complain that they don't have anything to talk about with their spouses, that just listening to the news on the radio while driving in the car or working around the house, can give you a whole host of topics to discuss," says Samantha, mother of a four-year-old son. "That's not very romantic, but it enables you to communicate on an adult level, rather than just talking about toilet training."

You can create a fun evening for yourselves in such a way that you become a couple again, not Joey's dad or Janie's mom. One couple I know always starts off their evening studying the wine list and discussing the various wines they have and haven't tried. Another couple pretends they are on their honeymoon and hold hands as much as possible. Still another couple pretends they are on their first date.

My husband and I always start off with a toast to our love for each other—and to getting out of the house successfully. If you are not exactly sure what to toast to, Paul Dickson has put together a wonderful compendium of toasts in his book called, *Toasts: The Complete Book of the Best Toasts, Sentiments, Blessings, Curses, and Graces* (Delacourte Press, 1981).

Again, I can't emphasize enough that parents need to allow themselves to have fun, to laugh and to enjoy themselves. One woman related to me that she and her husband went to the movies once in the summertime and she wore her mini-skirt *sans* underwear. "He put his hand on my leg and I whispered in his ear, 'You can go higher if you want,' " revealed Cathy. "It was a weeknight and there weren't a lot of people there. But it's those little surprises that have made our dates fun together. Sometimes we look at each other and say, 'My gosh, are we thirty-five years old or what?' Sometimes we act like teen-agers, but we feel great!"

Feeling and being sexy, and creating romantic times can be a terrific antidote for restlessness and discontent. When couples make the time and effort to generate enthusiasm and vitality in their relationship, they can build a powerfully intimate connection, one that combines a mature love with a young, romantic love.

Points to Remember

1. Show your spouse how much you appreciate him or her. Husbands, say 'thank you' when your wife has remembered to pick up your shirts at the cleaners. Wives, tell your husband how much you appreciate his help in the kitchen. A little appreciation goes a long way toward making each other feel good, and stimulating an interest in being romantic.

2. Nurture your spouse. Surprising each other with a cup of coffee or a shoulder massage draws you closer and can help put you in the mood for sex.

3. Dare to be intimate! Talk to your spouse directly about your feelings, and be an empathetic listener when your mate is brave enough to be vulnerable with you. Make an effort to look and be attractive to your spouse. Keep up your appearance. Find interesting subjects to talk about. *Never* stop courting your spouse!

7
Brief Encounters

Being Spontaneous
When Spontaneity Seems Gone

Whenever I take my daughters out for a drive in the car, even if we are just going to the grocery store, they become my best tour guides. "Look at those boats, Mommy!" my younger daughter will say, with wild and carefree enthusiasm. "Mom, look at that big dog hanging his head out the window," laughs my older daughter. As is typical behavior for most children, they do their share of fighting and whining, but overall, they have taught my husband and me something about life that is truly wonderful, and that has ironically helped to keep the spark of our love burning bright. They have shown both of us the joy that can be obtained by appreciating life's simple pleasures, and by allowing ourselves to *be spontaneous*.

Frequently, when couples become parents, they feel that spontaneity goes right out the window, and to a certain extent they are right. Once we become parents, we can no longer dash out to a nearby restaurant whenever we feel like it, or make love in the living room at high noon. But having children in the house does not mean we have to abandon spontaneity and put sensual pleasures on hold until the kids leave home. In fact, spontaneity is possible if you are willing to *be spontaneous*!

In order to have spontaneity, you have to be willing to make the effort to create the opportunity for it, or take advantage of the opportunity when it presents itself. Parents are lovers with one big disadvantage that lovers without kids rarely encounter: Time is not always on their side. Some parents might even say that time is *never* on their side. However, you can make some time and also use the little time you do have to be lovers. By learning to appreciate the few precious moments you do get with each other, those brief encounters can be very arousing and energizing.

Several couples I interviewed told me that they jump in the shower together and make quick, sensual love before the children wake up. One couple who has been married sixteen years, with three children, has had to learn to be spontaneous due to the husband's work schedule. He works nights and his wife works days, so they must juggle the few moments they can grab. "If I can get one of the kids in bed, another one to take a shower and the third child to busy himself doing his homework, that gives my wife and me fifteen or twenty minutes free to make love before I have to go to work," related Bryan.

Another father with four children found a way to make that transition time between work and home, spontaneous and fun. "Sometimes I come home from work and just want to be with my wife, so I'll whisper in her ear, 'Meet me in the garage in ten minutes,'" revealed Jim. "Paula thought this was weird, at first, but she got the kids settled with dinner, put her diaphragm in, and met me in the garage. Making love this way is sometimes a real challenge, but our sex life is not dull."

Other couples have created the time to be playful. "Once we parked in an empty grocery store parking lot to neck on our way home from a date," recalled Debbie, married fifteen-and-a-half years with two children, seven and nine.

Another mother of four children, ages six through twelve, related this story: "We were just driving down the highway and the urge hit, so we went down this country road where we used to go parking, when we first started dating. We pulled over to the side of the road and made love," says Jane. "I felt like a teen-ager again. It was really a lot of fun!"

Still another mother, happily married for twenty-five years, with five children, ages nine to twenty-one, told me this story: "One night, my husband and I were both exhausted. He got into his pajamas and plopped into bed before I did. Ten minutes later I flopped on the bed next to him with all my clothes on, including my shoes. He sat up, startled, and asked, 'Aren't you going to take off your clothes?' 'No,' I told him. 'That's *your* job!'" According to Tammy, her little stunt generated enough of a spark to jar them both out of being too tired for sex.

Instead of having a baby sitter come to the house, several couples I interviewed take their children to the baby sitter's home or to a neighbor's house, so they can go home and make love. "Sometimes, my husband and I go to a movie first, then go home and make love, then pick up our two sons at my neighbor's house," explained Julie.

LIFE'S SPONTANEOUS OPPORTUNITIES!

♥ Discuss your thoughts and feelings about spontaneity with your spouse. You may not feel like making love every time you get the chance, but you both might be interested in the possibility of having sex on a Saturday afternoon when your kids are at the neighbor's house, for example. By discussing the issue ahead of time, you can better prepare yourselves for your mini-adventure.

♥ Allow Grandma or Aunt Mary to spend some time with your children when she comes to visit. If she offers to stroll the baby to the park, take her up on her offer. As soon as she leaves, run up to your bedroom and take advantage of the time you have to be together. Avoid going over to the sink to clean the dirty lunch dishes, or to the laundry room to put a load of clothes in the dryer. The dishes and clothes will always be there, but golden opportunities won't.

♥ Create your own spontaneous rendezvous. Dare to be adventurous once in a while. You might sit down and do some fantasizing together about how and where you would make love: when your baby is playing happily in his or her playpen; when your kids are watching television; when you go to that drive-in movie and begin to feel like wild and crazy teen-agers again. Just fantasizing together will stimulate ideas and excitement.

"I have two or three neighbors I can call at a moment's notice, and they can call on me. We have an understanding that we are free to say, 'No, I can't baby-sit tonight,' and no one's feelings are hurt. When we are able, which is often, we do help each other out. It's a great system."

Still other parents have created opportunities to be together by setting their alarm clocks to go off earlier, and making love before the children wake up. "My husband will wake up first, roll over and whisper in my ear, 'Do you want to make mad, passionate love?' That's usually enough to arouse me, and we make love," related Tracy, mother of a four-year-old daughter and six-month-old son. "We will also make love sometimes after the kids are in bed, in the living room. What keeps our sex life from getting too routine is making love in different areas of the house. My husband will also get real playful and whisper in my ear, 'I can hardly wait until we are together.'"

"MY MOST SPONTANEOUS MOMENT!"

- ♥ Dale: "We went to a concert in the woods and when it was over, my wife and I walked over to this lagoon, went under some trees and made love."

- ♥ Cheryl: "I was folding some clothes one night in the laundry room after the kids went to sleep and my husband came downstairs. We started kissing, then got real passionate, and ended up making love on the laundry room floor!"

- ♥ Tony: "My wife and I were driving home from a friend's house one night and started talking about how horny we were. As soon as I could, I pulled over to the side of the road and we had some of the best sex we've had in years!"

- ♥ Kari: "My husband and I went to a drive-in movie, parked in the very last row and made love through the whole movie."

- ♥ Bill: "We have a roomy bathroom, and one morning when my wife and I were getting ready for work we just locked the door and made love on the bathroom floor. We had so much fun, that it's often part of our morning routine!"

Couples have also told me they sneak in love pats here and there, steal kisses and just hold hands a lot. They joke often, and invent affectionate nicknames for each other. "One thing I learned when I was in Vietnam is, if you can joke around and be playful, this helps a great deal in easing the stresses of your life," says Bryan, the father who works nights.

Another mother found that being playful and spontaneous with her husband drew them closer. "Sometimes, my husband will grab my breasts when the kids have their backs turned, then pull away real fast," revealed Joanne, mother of a ten-year-old son, and two daughters, eight and five. "And sometimes I'll put my hand in his pants pocket and squeeze his buttocks. These kinds of things always mean a lot to me—acting like kids. It is so very important to allow yourself to enjoy being a child occasionally." Joanne, whose first marriage to an alcoholic husband ended in divorce, greatly appreciates the playfulness she and her second husband enjoy together. "There were so many years in my life when I pushed all the playfulness out, thinking I was just too grown up for that. It's been nice discovering that my husband and I can derive small pleasures that come from being playful."

Nicknames conjure up pleasurable feelings as well. Couples who have private names for each other gain a great sense of security because they can be vulnerable and still feel loved. "After our son was born four years ago, we started with the nicknames," recalls Marti. "My husband Don and I called our son 'Doodle Boy,' then I started calling Don 'Doodle Dad,' and he began calling me 'Doodle Mom.' Now he calls me 'Doodles.'"

Another playful couple call each other "Mamma" and "Papa." This same couple also has other nicknames. The wife calls her husband "Superman" because one night they were having sex and her husband, who is over six feet tall, nearly broke the bed. "My daughter dubbed him that several years ago when she was sixteen years old," says Leah. "She heard us fooling around and then heard a big bang and thought the bed was falling down. He calls me 'Ten' because he thinks I have a perfect body."

To be spontaneous, you do not have to be perfect, rich or tremendously successful. You can obtain some sense of freedom when you *give yourself permission to be free*, and do not drag yourself down with such phrases as, "I should be cleaning the floor," or "I should be washing the car," instead of having some fun. Learn to appreciate those things that are positive in your life. *Capture ordinary moments and turn them into special events.* Most importantly, allow yourself to take the chance and risk being silly sometimes. By sharing yourself with your spouse, you encourage the opportunity to be intimate. When you uncover the emotional part of your relationship, you increase your chances of discovering the passionate side, as well.

> *"Intimate play is one of the ways that couples bring into the relationship the deepest parts of themselves; through playing with another you learn how to approach your partner's most intimate self."* [1]
> —Dr. William Betcher, psychologist and author of
> *Intimate Play: Creating Romance in Everyday Life*

> *"Open communication. . . can help sustain the emotional and sexual intensity of a relationship because it enables mates to discuss emotionally loaded taboo subjects. The emotional intensity enhances the general level of arousal, which heightens sexual arousal, which makes sex more exciting."* [2]
> —Dr. Ayala M. Pines, researcher

One mother I spoke to told me: "Sex can be anything you want it to be as long as you can communicate it." In discussing playfulness and spontaneity, an appreciation of ordinary life must also be included. We have a tendency to be always thinking about the future, which clouds our awareness of the present. As parents, it is easy to get into a "future fantasizing rut." "When we take that trip to Hawaii without the children and I am not feeling exhausted, then my spouse and I can be lovers," said one mother. This reminds me of the story of the couple who kept thinking they would be great lovers and get to know each other again once the kids went to college. When the last child was finally college bound, they drove him to his school in another state, came home to an empty house and realized they no longer had anything in common.

Parents who manage to keep the spark of their love alive make playful celebrations out of daily life. A good example of this is something a friend of mine did, when she and her husband could not afford a trip to Hawaii. She brought Hawaii to him. When her husband came home from work, he opened the front door to discover his wife in a grass skirt, an Aloha shirt and a lei around her neck. Hawaiian music was playing in the background and there were blown up palm trees around. She had drawn a bath for him and put fragrant flowers in the water. Even the children participated, by cutting up decorations and arranging pineapple slices on a plate.

Her efforts stirred up such wonderful feelings and after the children were in bed, she and her spouse had plenty of energy for sex. This is an elaborate example, but small gestures, such as getting up very early one morning a week to have a special breakfast—just the two of you—can mean a lot. One couple I know, rises at five o'clock in the morning, spreads out their best linen tablecloth, puts their fine china and some flowers on the table, and enjoys good coffee and pastries, before the children wake up. They pretend they are on vacation in a classy hotel. The idea is that when we try something different and let the child in us come out, we take a break from routine and are able to view our surroundings and our partners with fresh eyes.

HOW TO MAKE SEX EXCITING AGAIN

"One Saturday evening in June, my husband Kyle and I put on this high school graduation party for my son Ron," recalled Barbara. "My son and his friend had lined our long driveway with these candles inside cans. And we had decorated the house so nice. The party went very well, and we were so pleased with the whole event. After it was over, before we went to bed, Kyle and I held hands and took turns blowing the candles out one by one along the driveway. Then we sat on our deck for a while, drank coffee and just enjoyed being happy."

Kyle and Barbara could have asked their son to take care of putting out the candles and just gone to sleep because it had been a busy day and they were exhausted. Instead, they took each other by the hand and slowly, lovingly, blew out the candles themselves, then sat on their deck and shared a warm, moonlit night. *This is spontaneity—the idea being that we take advantage of opportunities to be lovers when situations present themselves.*

One of the several questions I asked couples was: If you feel spontaneity remains, how have you and your spouse found ways to be spontaneous? The answers I received from parents who responded to this item were very encouraging. Many parents felt that spontaneity was reduced or changed, but not gone. One enthusiastic father of four had this to say: "Sexual spontaneity could and should be a part of every relationship no matter how many children you have. Share yourself with your partner, even if you only have a few minutes to get naked and make love. Being able to give yourself to your lover is the greatest therapy there is!" Another father of three children, four, eight and eleven said: "Just seize whatever opportunity arises. Remind the kids that their favorite television show is on, or suggest a play activity." And a mom of three active daughters urged: "Think fast when the opportunity presents itself."

SEXY WAYS TO BE SPONTANEOUS WHEN. . .

♥ your kids are watching television. . .

♥ your kids go over to a neighbor's house to play. . .

♥ your baby sitter takes your baby out for a stroll, or your children to the park. . .

♥ your child takes a nap. . .

♥ your children are still asleep in the early morning. . .

♥ your children have finally gone to sleep for the night. . .

"My responsibilities have increased dramatically since I became a parent, but I learned that if your priorities are really clear and you make having fun together one of the most important aspects of your relationship, this keeps your love life exciting," related a mother of three children, ages four, six and eight. "We always find time to hug, kiss and make love."

Whether you take a bath together, make love in your living room or pinch each other's bottoms, these ideas are all wonderful ways to keep the spark alive. If you are among the parents who finds yourself saying such things as: "Our loss of spontaneity has occurred due to our heightened sense of responsibility for our children and attention to their needs; I regret the loss," or "Because my spouse always puts the kids first before our relationship, we don't have time for each other any more," then you need to sit down and rethink your priorities and expectations.

When we become parents, a strange thing happens, which most of us are not aware of. As sex therapist Dagmar O'Connor explains: "We identify our spouses with our parents—wife with mother, husband with father—and then we find that we do not feel very much like making love to them." [3] We unconsciously embroil our psyches in the Oedipus complex and incest taboo, the turmoil we wrestled with as children when we learned, subconsciously, to turn off our sexual feelings for our mothers and fathers. This is part of our normal development says O'Connor—to turn off sexually to our parents and siblings in the family we are born into. When we marry and create our own family, however, those taboos resurface to haunt us. "*We once again turn off to our loved one*—our husband or wife," says O'Connor. She continues: "*Family love precludes sexual love. The one person we have chosen to love and make love to for the rest of our life is the one person we have often 'learned' to turn off to.*" [4]

Not only do we inhibit ourselves, but strangely enough, we also inhibit each other. No matter how spontaneous a couple has been prior to being married or before having children; after they have been married a while and even more so when children come along, they may have sex only on certain nights, in the same room in the same way. Gradually, they restrict each other's sexual behavior. Both husband and wife become afraid of expressing their needs because each is fearful of the other's disapproval.

For your own happiness, you must also lighten up about sex and not be afraid to try something new if boredom is killing your sex life. Lovemaking has, unfortunately, become far too serious a business, instead of the simple God-given pleasure it was meant to be between two people who are deeply committed to each other. Talk to each other about your desires; new lovemaking positions you would like to try, new places where you would like to make love, different times to make love—early morning, instead of late at night.

Rather than thinking you are strange or crazy, you might be surprised at how open and grateful your spouse may be that you are suggesting a tryst in your bathroom or in front of your fire place, to help both of you get out of your sexual rut.

"One impression I get from the forty hours a week I spend with my patients, week after week, is that the most neglected sexual art these days is laughter—true mirth. Few couples seem aware of the aphrodisia of laughter—that can encourage and even prolong pleasure." [5]

—Dr. Avodah K. Offit, M.D., psychiatrist
and sex therapist

In talking with marriage counselors, one of the elements that they notice in troubled marriages is that couples have stopped having fun together. So relax; have fun! If the bed breaks down, or your kids wonder what Mom and Dad are doing in the bathroom, so what! Maybe they will end up calling you "Superman," "Superwoman" or "Super Lovers!"

CONQUER YOUR INHIBITIONS!

♥ Talk to your spouse and make a date with him or her to discuss your feelings. If this is difficult for you, write your request in a note, made up to look like an invitation.

♥ Pick a time to talk when it is quiet and you are free from distractions. If talking to your spouse about your sexual feelings is hard, write them down, and give the letter to your spouse to read. At least this will be a start toward breaking the ice. Refrain from using the "you" word, which insinuates blame and may put your spouse on the defensive. Use the "I" word, instead. For example, rather than saying: "You never want to try new positions," say, "I'd like to make love with you standing up in the shower, but I'm afraid you will think this is a silly idea." Your spouse can then feel more comfortable in expressing his or her feelings.

♥ Discuss your fears first, then you will find it is much easier to discuss your desires. You can each make up your own wish list, and call it: "Ten Crazy Ways I'd Like to Make Love with You!" Then talk about all the items on your list. Not only will you begin to feel more comfortable with each other about sex, but less fearful about trying out your ideas.

Winning the Battle against Sexual Boredom

When talking about spontaneity, I am also talking about variety. Interjecting variety into your sex life is one of the most important offenses against boring sex, or no sex at all. The importance of introducing variety into a relationship can't be emphasized enough by researchers who have done extensive studies regarding boredom in a marriage. Dr. Ayala Pines, for example, believes that the greater the variety in a relationship, the lower the levels of burnout. Says Pines: "Variety can be found somewhere on the happy ground between overload and boredom. People function best at an optimal level of variety. Extremely high levels of variety create anxiety and strain, while extremely low levels create boredom and anger. The optimal level is different for different people and requires constant and continuous stimulation from the environment. This is why no matter how exciting a marriage is initially, in the absence of variety, boredom and monotony can wear it down." [6] According to Pines, further data show ". . . that the more variety there is in a marriage, the better the couple describe their sex life. On the flip side, the more boredom, the poorer the quality of sex." [7]

There are many ways couples increase emotional arousal and rejuvenate romance in their relationship. Foremost in their thinking, of course, is the attitude that it is all right to be playful and spontaneous. For one couple I know, it means going skinny-dipping in their hot tub after their daughter has gone to bed. For another couple it means playing their own special game they call "Mummy," where the woman's husband slowly takes off each article of her clothing until he finds her smooth body underneath. And for still another couple, it means making love in the laundry room on top of the dryer while it is running.

"One night, after the kids had gone to bed, my husband and I were lying on the sofa in our living room watching a football game and one thing led to another," related Pam, mother of two children, ten and four. "We started making love, which was really unplanned and very relaxed. We were laughing and having a great time. It just seemed right."

Still another couple threw their cares to the wind, when they made love inside their screened-in porch during an especially hot summer evening. "Being spontaneous like that was really satisfying and special," said John, father of two young daughters.

Parents I have spoken to tell me that frequently they think about being spontaneous. They fantasize about it and greatly desire it, but do nothing about it for fear of appearing silly to their spouse. If they finally do communicate their feelings, more often than not, the listening spouse loves the idea. "We were walking alone on the beach at Assateague Island, Virginia, in an area where there were no other people around and the thought of making love was running through our minds, but we didn't communicate it and missed a terrific opportunity," Peter said, the father of three teen-agers. His wife Amy felt the same regret: "We kicked ourselves when we got back home and realized we had both thought about doing the same thing, but didn't talk to each other about it."

Nothing in sex is silly, crazy or stupid if it is done with love, respect and understanding for each other. In addition to being fun, developing a sense of playfulness in your relationship can help ease the tension when it is difficult for you to tell your spouse about your desires and needs.

Playing for Keeps

At the same time you must be tuned into opportunities for lovemaking and grab them when they arise, you must also be willing to work at creating some moments of pleasure. If you wait around for sexual inspiration to hit, you may be waiting a long time. Couples who have a sense of spontaneity and playfulness in their marriages tell me they constantly put forth the effort to make these elements an integral part of their intimacy. In addition, being "keepers of the flame," is something they *both* do. They do not consider keeping the spark alive the "woman's job," or the "man's job." In fact, it almost becomes a friendly competition with these couples at times, as each spouse tries to outdo the other with surprises. One woman outdid herself one day when she visited the Erotic Baker, a bakery in New York City that sells pastries shaped like sex parts, and naked men and women making love. She bought pastry for her doctor husband, which was a cake shaped like a man with no clothes on except for a stethoscope. She waited until after the kids were in bed, then shared it with her spouse while they drank their coffee. The coffee got cold, while things heated up in the kitchen.

A father I spoke to who frequently does the grocery shopping for his wife in the evening, told me he sometimes brings home flowers and a six-pack of beer with the diapers. Another father told me he approaches his wife at bedtime with the words "hook up." This phrase means that it is time for her to stand behind him and put her arms around his waist. Then they go chugging off to bed together like a choo-choo train. Still another father told me that he and his wife have a game they like to play called, "Chase," where they run after each other in their bedroom stark naked. They also play another game called "Heads or Tails," with a quarter, and the person who loses has to jump into bed first to warm it up.

When these couples plan weekends away together, *sans* children, they carry their playfulness with them. One mother I spoke to says she and her husband pretend they are on their honeymoon. "We just do whatever we feel like, which sometimes means we stay in bed all day," explained Marion, who has a six-year-old son. Another couple pretends they are meeting each other for the first time. Still another couple plays a game they call, "Don Juan and the Mistress."

Being playful and spontaneous involves the ability of two people to be inventive, and relaxed enough to let go, just for a little while. By allowing yourselves to connect emotionally and physically in this way, you are cultivating a sense of flexibility, which may help ease the daily stresses that can lead to sexual boredom and apathy. At the same time, you are strengthening the bond of love between the two of you, and making room for emotional growth. An additional benefit to this carefree behavior is that you are also building a lot of happy memories, which makes for a truly intimate relationship.

Points to Remember

1. To have spontaneity in your life, you have to be willing to make the effort to create the opportunity for it, or take advantage of the opportunity when it presents itself.

2. Spontaneous play, such as joking with each other, calling each other affectionate nicknames, chasing or tickling each other, can add a special spark to your relationship.

3. Give yourself permission to be a little wild and crazy sometimes. Avoid dragging yourself down with endless "I shoulds," i.e., "I should be cleaning the floor," or "I should be cutting the grass." Give yourself a chance to say, "I *will* take thirty minutes off to have fun!" Learn to appreciate the positive aspects of your life.

8

"More Passion, Please!"

How to Put the *Fun* Back into Your Sex Life

When asked specifically about their sex lives, many mothers and fathers revealed that sex is boring and routine. For some parents sex is problematic and even non-existent. "It's the same old in and out! He often comes too quickly and I'm left unsatisfied," one mother told me. "We have sex in the same way, in the same place and usually at the same time; there's no variation," said a frustrated father. "I would like more foreplay, more experimenting, more help in reaching orgasm," expressed another mother. Still another father complained about always having to initiate sex, and about the fact that there was no experimenting: "We never have oral sex. That really bothers me." And still another mother said: "I would like to make more noise, but I am afraid the kids will hear us."

Parents feel exhausted from working all week long, either inside or outside the home. They have very little privacy, and very little time, so it is easy to see how sex can become routine and boring and just no fun. Add to these problems the inhibitions and feelings of guilt and frustration stemming from a lack of accurate sexual knowledge when they were growing up, and you have sexual difficulties and much unhappiness.

> *"There is little question that personal dissatisfaction with sex is commonplace in our society today. Half of all American marriages are troubled by some form of sexual distress ranging from disinterest and boredom to outright sexual dysfunction. The sexual problems people encounter the most frequently are inhibitions and guilt, performance anxiety, erotic boredom, and blind acceptance of sexual misinformation or myths. . . these four problems collectively account for more than eighty percent of the sexual dissatisfactions in modern American society."* [1]
>
> —Masters and Johnson, founders of the Masters and Johnson Institute

Granted, it is hard to feel sexual when you have been taking care of the baby who eats and spits up all day, or when you have had a long hard day at the office, but as you discover ways to explore your sexuality and pleasure yourselves, you will be able to experience a renewed "sexual energy" and "sexual enjoyment." As for dealing with inhibitions, guilt and anxieties from our past, Bernie Zilbergeld, Ph.D., in his excellent book, *Male Sexuality: A Guide to Sexual Fulfillment,* offers hope and encouragement when he says: "What has been learned can be unlearned and replaced by more personally appropriate knowledge. Actually, you don't really have to unlearn anything. All you need to do is recognize what is getting in your way and loosen its grip just a little bit. Much of sex therapy, and much of what occurs in workshops and courses on sex, is simply the use of techniques designed to gently unleash you from some of your early sexual learning. . ." [2]

In this chapter, I will show you how to conquer these sexual myths; how to think beyond the stereotypical distortions regarding genitals and sex, and how to correct the misinformation that has polluted our view of our own sexuality. I will also offer suggestions that will help you to accept and express your sexuality better and make sex fun.

Sexuality, unfortunately, is too complex for quick fixes. It is a shame we somehow cannot take some sort of vitamin pill and solve all our sexual hang-ups. But you can help yourself right now: by

ACCEPT YOUR SEXUALITY BY SAYING TO YOURSELF

♥ "I have a right to feel like a sexy, worthwhile person."

♥ "My body is beautiful because it is uniquely me. I am unique."

♥ "It is perfectly all right to explore my own body, to discover which sensations feel good and which ones don't."

♥ "It is perfectly all right for me to talk to my partner about sex. Talking about my needs and desires, and being sensitive and understanding to my spouse's needs, will help us to make our sex life better."

♥ "It is perfectly all right to try new sexual positions, or incorporate sexual fantasy, sex toys or erotica into our sexual relationship, as long as this is done with love and understanding, and we do not hurt each other."

realizing that good sex involves obtaining accurate sex information; a willingness to talk to your spouse about your sexual needs, fears, anxieties and displeasures; and the desire to take some risks, to explore with your lover the various options available for creative sexual expression.

After conducting extensive research in the area of sexuality, it seems that a lack of accurate sex information is at the heart of our sexual dissatisfactions. How frustrating is a lack of accurate sex information? According to Shere Hite, author of *The Hite Report on Female Sexuality* (Dell, 1976) and director of Hite Research International and Lonnie Barbach, Ph.D., psychologist and sex therapist, more than half of American women say they prefer clitoral to vaginal stimulation to reach orgasm, for example, yet many men and women were led to believe otherwise, due to cruel distortions in romance literature, some sexual psychology and traditional male folk wisdom. Folklore and myths have convinced people that women will have an orgasm only through vaginal stimulation. In actuality, however, the majority of women experience orgasm through clitoral stimulation. Barbach notes in her lectures that: "The vast majority of women are as frustrated by this as men would be if they thought they were supposed to reach orgasm by having their testicles rubbed." [3]

Growing up, many of us were told very little about sex. We learned bits and pieces of information passed along by embarrassed parents and teachers. In many cases, our sex education consisted of "juicy secrets" passed along through the "peer grapevine." "A lot of adults today are still very naive about their sexuality," says Joani Blank, a sex therapist and sex educator in San Francisco. "Everybody assumes that kids and adolescents have a lot to learn about sexuality because they are kids, but with adults, it's a different story. Because they are uptight about sex to begin with, they are *mortified* that they have gotten to be twenty-five, or thirty-five or forty-five years old and still don't know, for example, what the clitoris is for, because *nobody ever told them!*"

Indeed, it is my fondest hope that upon completing the reading of this chapter, you will be inclined to pursue the sexual information you need and want in order to feel good about your sexuality, and to create the mutually satisfying sex life that you desire.

SUCCESSFUL WAYS TO FLIRT, FOR BETTER SEX, NOW!

- ♥ Look your spouse in the eye and give him or her a compliment.
- ♥ Whisper "I love you!" in your spouse's ear.
- ♥ Kiss your spouse on the neck.
- ♥ Grab your spouse's hand and hold it the way you used to.
- ♥ Squeeze your husband's buttocks, or touch your wife's breasts when the kids aren't looking.
- ♥ Give your spouse a five-minute shoulder massage.

In responding to my questionnaire, parents were incredibly open in regard to what bothered them about their sex lives. I am grateful for those insights. At the same time I wanted to say to each of them: "Don't tell me; *tell your spouse!*" Unfortunately, when we are upset about the way our spouse makes love, or doesn't make love, or about our own sexual feelings, we tend to almost become comatose. We think that something is wrong with us, or our spouse, or that this is a situation we just have to live with or hide or both.

But it doesn't have to be this way. In many instances, nothing is wrong with you. The problems may develop simply from a lack of accurate sex information and communication, something that can easily be remedied in most cases. Many parents I spoke to who claim to have a satisfying sex life, tell me they had to work at overcoming their fears and inhibitions to make sex satisfying. You can, too!

HOW TO FIND YOUR SEXUAL SELF

As Dr. Zilbergeld points out, you have to find out what is getting in your way, emotionally, and then loosen its grip on you, in order to free your sexual self. Were you told that sex is dirty or bad? Were you made to feel that your body is something you should hide? Were you told that sex is for reproductive purposes only? Were you given the message that only bad girls have fun sex? Were you given the message that you don't fool around with good girls? One big way to help yourself and your relationship, is to talk about your sex education, or lack of it, with your spouse. You can ease tension, learn to talk about sex and begin to find solutions to your problems by first, *telling your story.* Here are some stories parents told me:

"In our house sex wasn't forbidden, it was *dirty*, just a dirty thing," recalled Sophie, mother of a girl, nine, and boy, twelve. "I remember asking my mom one time if you have to be married to have a baby and she said, 'No.' That was it! Just 'No.' If I ever asked her a question about sex, she would answer me honestly, but briefly. The message I got was, 'Don't ask me that!' So anything I learned about sex I learned on my own. When I was older and started dating, it was all play-by-ear for me. If I had a date with a boy and he started playing with my breasts, it scared me, but I figured this is what you do. Today, I still feel like I'm hindered by this "sex is dirty" message. I'd love to rush up to my husband at the end of the day, be real passionate and take him into the bedroom and make love, but something always holds me back."

"The one thing my mother always told me about sex was 'never trust a man,'" related Betsy, the mother of two sons, ten and thirteen. "This is a message I am still trying to get over today."

John, the father of a daughter, six, and son, eight, told me about his introduction to sex education: "My parents never really talked about sex at all, so I learned about it in the back seat of a car. When I was going to Catholic school, the priest would come talk to us once a week about the ten commandments and about not coveting your neighbor's wife. If I asked him questions about sex, his answers were always vague and skirted the issue."

Diane, the mother of two sons, one and four, related: "I hardly ever saw my mother naked, unless it was a big mistake. So I got the definite impression from her that you should hide yourself and be real embarrassed if anyone saw you naked. I grew up with this fear of anyone seeing me without my clothes on. I am still embarrassed to a certain extent. When I found out what you had to do to make a baby, I thought to myself, 'Well, I guess if I want to have children I suppose I could bear to have sex three or four times.' The awakenings of my sexual desire were so suppressed that now I feel basically like a plant that's been tied down."

Terri, the mother of twin, five-year-old daughters, recalled a strange notion about penises: "My biggest misconception that I carried all through high school was that penises were cold, slimy things. A male friend and I were talking about that once and he got very embarrassed, looked down at the floor and said, 'Well, they aren't *really* cold and slimy.' I felt badly about putting him on the spot like that, but I still carried around this idea until I got to college."

You may not be able to get rid of these silly, hurtful notions overnight. It may take a lot of talking and the ability to *make connections* between past hurts and current troubles, and realize that you can change things. In some cases, obtaining accurate sex information may solve your problem. In other cases, especially if you are feeling unable to solve the problem yourself, you may want to consult with a marriage or family counselor or sex therapist. Telling your spouse your story, like these parents told me, expressing any hurts, anger, resentments, and listening with empathy when your spouse tells you his or her story, is a good place to start.

While many people think that sex is something that is just a natural instinct, like "Me, Tarzan, You, Jane," human sexuality is basically a learned phenomenon, says Bernie Zilbergeld, Ph.D., author of *Male Sexuality: A Guide to Sexual Fufillment.* "Very little of our sexual behavior can properly be called instinctive. . . It is easy to assume that since we, like all animals, are programmed to continue our species, intercourse would occur without learning. But the issue is much more complex. . . The ideas that some ways of having sex are

---

THREE WAYS TO BEGIN TO TELL YOUR STORY

♥ Accept your feelings. As I said before, sad, scary or angry feelings are not bad feelings, and you are not a bad person for feeling them. Feelings are a part of who we are as people. And when you accept your feelings, you accept yourself.

♥ Try to understand your feelings. The better you can understand why you are feeling what you are feeling, the sooner you can begin to solve your problems. If dealing with your feelings is too difficult or frightening to handle on your own, there is absolutely nothing wrong with seeking the help of a professional counselor. The American Association of Sex Educators, Counselors, and Therapists offers listings for certified sex therapists nationwide: (312) 644-0828.

♥ Express your feelings. If a fear of rejection stands in your way of expressing your feelings, realize that this is a normal feeling. You can help conquer it by saying something to your spouse like: "I want to tell you about this, but I am afraid you will reject me, or not understand. I want to talk to you about my feelings because I want us to be closer, but I am afraid." Rather than allowing your fear to isolate you, *use it* to make your emotional connection with your spouse.

---

better than others, that certain actions are decent while others are indecent. . . all these are products of learning." [4]

Defining sexuality is a bit complex because so many different, sometimes distorted definitions, have been attached to the word. In the opinion of Masters and Johnson, sexuality has a broad meaning ". . .since it refers to all aspects of being sexual. Sexuality means a dimension of personality instead of referring to a person's capacity for erotic response alone." [5]

Our sexuality is part of who we are as people, an aspect of ourselves that should not be ignored or repressed, but should be allowed to be "celebrated" within marriage. Our sexuality, and our children's sexuality, is not something we can shove under the rug or cut out of our bodies.

In spite of some considerable anxiety, many parents today are making concerted efforts to offer open, honest and accurate information to their children about sex. They don't want their children to suffer from sexual hang-ups the way they have suffered. By being open parents, and giving their children accurate information in a frank, honest manner, they are doing their children and themselves a great service. In fact, very often when parents check out books at

---

TEN STEPS TO GIVING EACH OTHER A SENSUOUS BATH

♥ Treat your bath as a special ritual.

♥ Prepare your sensual place: put some soft romantic music in your portable cassette player; light a candle; arrange special bath soaps and towels near the tub; get a bath pillow to put behind your lover's head; get rid of the kiddie bath toys; and pour a glass of champagne or a non-alcoholic beverage.

♥ Turn on the water, and while it is running, invite your lover near the tub, and slowly, lovingly remove each article of clothing.

♥ Give each other gentle, light kisses all over while you are removing your lover's clothes, then have your lover slowly remove your clothes.

♥ Slip into the tub, and take turns lathering each other up. Go slow and enjoy the sensation of the soap gliding over smooth skin.

♥ Take turns sitting behind each other and holding each other when you are in the tub. For example, your husband can slide into the tub behind you, with his legs surrounding your buttocks. He can lather your neck, shoulders, back and breasts. Later, you can change places and get behind your husband, and lather his neck, back, chest and any other delicious parts you desire.

♥ Take turns sipping the champagne from the same glass.

♥ Rub each other dry, then either rub each other with talcum powder if it is a warm evening, or with lotion.

♥ Embrace while still naked.

♥ Look each other in the eye and say, "I Love You."

---

the library or buy books for their children on sex, they begin reading these books and learn new facts themselves! You are never too old to learn and explore, especially about an area that is so important.

By opening up to one another and seeking answers to questions about sex for themselves, parents are learning to be the sensual lovers they want to be. One mother, who finally got up enough courage to make her needs known, was surprised to see how willing her husband was to help her get her needs met. She was finally able to achieve orgasms thanks to her own courage and her husband's attentiveness. Another mother said: "My husband is more aware of my body and what feels best. He is more daring and concerned with my pleasure. We are both more giving now." And a father said: "Our pleasure with each other's bodies continues to expand and increase with age as we learn to talk more and share more." In another marriage, laughter in sex took on a higher priority, as the couple allowed themselves to experiment with the variety of ways to please each other. "We laugh more and are less self-conscious," said the mother. "There is also a more spontaneous feeling about our lovemaking."

Become More Aware of Your Beautiful Body

It always amazes me to watch little babies and to see how free they are with their bodies. As doting parents, we have all kissed our babies' toes and eyelids, their hands and bellies. We develop a loving bond with our children through touch. As adults, in a loving relationship with our spouses, however, the art of touching—that would help us to develop a closer bond with our partner and help us to feel good about our bodies—has for many parents become a lost art. But touch is a good way to begin to discover your sexuality, your sensual self. By touching, I mean hugging, kissing, cuddling, caressing; not necessarily always leading to sexual intercourse. Rather than being a "means to an end," i.e. sexual intercourse, touch can be a wonderful way to communicate and celebrate your love.

"All kinds of sexual interactions are valid and significant," says sex therapist Joani Blank. "They have meaning and their meaning is not completely lost if a couple does not complete some kind of sexual act, such as intercourse or orgasms for both partners. I've had some people come to me and say, 'I haven't had sex in six months,' and I tell them, 'If you count all those things you have been doing such as necking or petting that aren't intercourse as not *sex*, then you are right. You haven't had sex in six months. But if you say you get turned on by touching each other's genitals for five minutes, then you've had sex!'"

You can get in touch with your sexual self in a number of ways: dancing close; kissing, petting or necking; slowly taking each other's clothes off; washing each other in a sensual bath; giving each other a massage. The art of being sensual has to do with attitude; being gentle and slow moving. "Sensuality is the appreciation of all the sensory modes; flavor, fragrance, hue, texture, timbre, contour and more," relates Dr. Kenneth Ray Stubbs, a sensate therapist, internationally known for pioneering the use of massage techniques in sex therapy. "A sensuous lover is willing to take the time." [6]

A good way to get in touch with your body and feel sensual is through massage. Dr. Stubbs offers two books on this subject: *Romantic Interludes: A Sensuous Lovers Guide* (Secret Garden, 1988) and *Erotic Massage: The Touch of Love* (Secret Garden, 1989). Three other good books on massage are: *The Massage Book*, by George Downing (Random House, 1972). *The Art of Sensual Massage*, by Gordon Inkeles & Murray Todris (Simon & Schuster, 1972), includes sensual photographs. *Touching for Pleasure*, by Adele Kennedy and Susan Dean, Ph.D. (Chatsworth Press, 1986), includes a discussion of oral sex. If you would rather follow massage techniques on video, Dr. Stubbs offers video tapes that complement both his massage books: Volume I, which includes general sensual massage techniques and other ways to pleasure the senses, and Volume II, which includes genital massage. You can get these books and videos at sexuality boutiques, which I include at the end of this chapter.

Whether you are giving your lover a back massage, or caressing the genital region, which is highly sensitive to touch, learning specific massage techniques that can relax and arouse your lover can be quite helpful toward establishing a better intimacy connection and stimulating sexual enjoyment.

Being sensual and creating a sensual environment for you and your lover actually takes very little effort. Mostly, it involves accepting your body and accepting pleasure, not feeling as though you have to *earn* the pleasure. You have a right to feel, to enjoy and to *give* pleasure, as well.

A READING LIST OF EROTICA

♥ *Erotic by Nature: A Celebration of Life, of Love, and of Our Wonderful Bodies*, edited by David Steinberg (Shakti Press/Red Adler Books, 1988). A collection of duotone photographs, drawings, short stories and poems. The erotic material is honest, intimate, playful and interjects an emotional warmth that is passionate and provocative without being pornographic.

♥ *Erotic Art of the Masters: The 18th, 19th and 20th Centuries*, by Bradley Smith.*

♥ *Eros in Antiquity*, color photographs by Antonia Mulas, depicting erotic art from the "Golden Ages" of Greece and Pompeii.*

♥ *The Chinese Way of Love*, by Charles Humana and Wang Wu.*

♥ *Delta of Venus: Erotica* (Harcourt Brace Jovanovich, 1977) and *Little Birds, Erotica* (Harcourt Brace Jovanovich, 1979), both by Anaïs Nin.

♥ *Pleasures: Women Write Erotica*, by Lonnie Barbach, Ph.D. and Linda Levine (Harper & Row, 1985).

♥ *Erotic Interludes: Tales Told by Women*, edited by Lonnie Barbach, Ph.D. (Harper & Row, 1987).

♥ *Forbidden Flowers*, by Nancy Friday.*

♥ *My Secret Garden*, by Nancy Friday (Trident Press, 1973).

♥ *Fantasex: A Book of Erotic Games for the Adult Couple*, by Rolf Milonas (Putnam, 1975). Provocative games that are noncompetitive and non-adversarial.

♥ *The Playbook for Men about Sex* and *The Playbook for Women about Sex*, by Joani Blank (Down There Press, 1976).

♥ *Sexual Energy Extasy, A Guide to the Ultimate, Intimate Sexual Experience*, by David Alan and Ellen Jo Dorfman (Peakskill Publishing, 1985).

*These books are out of print. Look for them at your local used bookstore.

MAKING SEX FUN

Looking at erotica together, sharing sexual fantasies or playing with sex toys, are all valid ways to enhance pleasure. While I do not advocate pornography, some erotica shown in a healthy way can help create excitement in your relationship. Unfortunately, material such as this is not easy to find. More often, we are bombarded by distorted representations of love. Since the process of choosing erotica, sharing sexual fantasies and introducing sex toys is so highly personal, I cannot tell you what to choose or do, but I can offer some suggestions, and ways to approach these areas with your spouse.

> *"Given the trend of the last fifteen years toward a greater acceptability and accessibility of sexually explicit items— and the recent boom in uncensored cable TV and home video systems—it seems important to gather more complete data on the effects of erotica. We should not overlook the possibility that the use of erotica is sometimes accompanied by problems; neither should we be frightened by old negative attitudes reborn in the guise of modern morality."* [7]
> —Drs. Masters and Johnson

Many parents feel embarrassed, funny, guilty or a little scared about introducing these areas of pleasure into their relationship because there is only one reason, for example, to watch erotic movies, and it is to get turned on. But again, there is nothing wrong with pleasing yourselves if it is done with love and respect for each other.

> *"Fear of sexuality leads to the belief that sex is bad and secrecy is good. The fact, however, is that these beliefs are destructive. . . Facing and letting go of sexual fear is a healthier, more life-affirming choice."* [8]
> —Marty Klein, marriage and sex therapist,
> author of *Your Sexual Secrets*

If you are not in the habit of looking at erotic material or reading erotic passages, but would like to introduce the idea of doing so with your spouse, a good way to begin is when you have some quiet time alone together, either in a restaurant, or at home after the children have gone to bed. Pick a time when you do not have some serious angry issue on the table to discuss, such as a financial problem or disagreement over disciplining the children. Then, start with your intention.

You might say: "You know, honey, I've really been wanting to feel closer to you sexually. I found this wonderful book of erotic fantasies and I would like to read some parts of it to you when we are in bed sometime. Is this the sort of thing you might be interested in?" Not: "How about we do this tonight?" but, "I was thinking about this general idea. What do you think?" The other person might say: "Yes, I think that might be fun." Then you could say: "That's great. Maybe this weekend we can get a chance to do that."

Reading sexually exciting poems or looking at sexually exciting art together just may add that little zing in your love life that you have been waiting for. Just don't let the kiddies see it. And if you get the giggles in bed, so what? Enjoy!

Sharing Sexual Fantasies

When I asked parents about their sexual fantasies they told me that they fantasize about a lot of things. For example, women related that they fantasized about making love with someone other than their spouse or with several men, or about being seduced by another man or several men, and even fantasizing what it would be like to make love with other women. The men said they fantasized about such things as watching someone else make love to their wives, group sex or seducing someone else into sexual relations. Both husbands and wives related that they fantasized about making love under

---

THREE WAYS TO CREATE YOUR OWN SEXUAL FANTASY

♥ Begin a story with your spouse. You might start by saying something like: "I slowly slipped off my red teddy. . ."

♥ Stop your story at an especially stimulating point, then let your spouse continue it.

♥ Take turns adding on to the story at especially exciting parts. Continue the story, until you both become so aroused you will want to create your own real life sex scene.

idyllic conditions, such as on a warm, secluded beach, or in a tropical paradise. Some spouses kept their fantasies to themselves. Some spouses shared them with each other. All of these fantasies are perfectly normal—just brief, make-believe escapes of the mind. The breakdown of trust and actual deterioration in a relationship that may occur when one of these fantasies is carried out could be disastrous. Neither the mothers or fathers had any desire to act on their fantasies, except to work on finding a baby sitter and booking a hotel room sometime, so they can create those idyllic conditions.

FIVE SEXUALITY BOUTIQUES

Joani Blank started her own sexuality, or vibrator store, as she prefers to call it, thirteen years ago. Her philosophy about her store, called Good Vibrations, 1210 Valencia Street, San Francisco, California 94110, (415) 550-0912 is basically this: "The inspiration for Good Vibrations grew out of my many years of experience as a sex therapist and educator. After working with hundreds of women—and dozens of men—I realized that many people would appreciate and benefit from a nice place to shop for sex toys and books. Good Vibrations reflects my desire to encourage and support honest communication about sex and my belief that better communication promotes health, intimacy, creativity, joy and equality of the sexes." Blank offers a mail order catalogue that includes information about various sex toys, which can be obtained from her store for $2.00, plus all the books I mentioned, which can be ordered through The Sexuality Library catalogue ($2.00).

Other boutiques, which offer catalogues or brochures of books on sexuality, plus lingerie, lotions and oils, vibrators, even sexuality workshops are: Loveseason, 4001-198th Street, S.W. Suite 7, Lynnwood, Washington 98036, (206) 775-4502; Eve's Garden International, LTD, 119 West 57th Street, Suite 1406, New York, New York 10019, (212) 757-8651; Come to Your Senses, 321 Cedar Avenue South, Minneapolis, Minnesota 55454, (612) 339-0050; The Erogenous Zone, 343 North State College Blvd., Fullerton, California 92631, (714) 879-3270.

For general information on human sexuality, sexuality and disability, AIDS education, etc., contact: SIECUS (Sex Information and Education Council of the U.S.), 32 Washington Place, New York, New York 10003.

"There are certain fantasies that we share when we are making love, but we don't discuss them at other times," says Rita, mother of a one-year-old daughter. "They are just fantasies, not part of our day-to-day life. We don't tell fantasies every time we make love; usually once every three times. If my husband has a fantasy he wants to share he will tell me about it, then say, 'What do you think of this one?' And I will say, 'Oh, that sounds good; let's use it next time.' Or, 'No, that one doesn't really turn me on, something else maybe.' "

Whether you choose to share a fantasy or not is your choice. Some spouses choose not to, but to play the fantasy in their heads during lovemaking. This is perfectly fine, too. For other parents, it is not so much the idea of sharing the fantasy that is a turn-on, but rather letting their spouses know that they think about sex. You might be walking down the street and see a gorgeous pink teddy in a boutique window, for example. You might then say to your husband: "Wouldn't that be great for when we go on our trip next month?" Or you might say to your wife: "I can't wait until we get a chance to make love."

Another way to turn each other on is to talk about a great sexual experience you shared in the past. For example, saying something like: "Do you remember when we found that old cabin in the woods and made love there?" This can heat things up as much as sharing a fantasy.

If you are feeling burned out sexually right now, and want to interject a little passion, sharing a sexual fantasy, desire or memory may "ignite your fire"!

Sex Toys

The myths surrounding the idea that incorporating sex toys, fragrant oils or ostrich feathers into your love relationship is somehow excessive, have prevented many couples from introducing variety into their lovemaking.

In fact, the tendency *not* to seek new and accurate information that might enhance your individual sexuality and love life, is a recipe for boredom. Relates William Betcher, Ph.D.: "To be bored with your sexual relationship, to feel 'there's nothing there' . . .usually means that you are cut off psychologically from the deepest sources of your erotic life. Play allows you to experiment with erotic alternatives. . ." [9] For those who may feel that the very idea of sex play is somehow degenerate, Betcher emphasizes: "The very essence of play is its creative unpredictability. You're not stuck in one mode, genital or otherwise. A lifetime of making love in the missionary position can be as much a perversion as a fondness for women's shoes." [10]

Parents who use ostrich feathers, for example, told me that this sex toy does help break up a routine sex life. "We got ostrich feathers as a curiosity item to start with," related Bill. "It hasn't become a regular part of our sex life, but we use and enjoy them on occasion."

How does one find out more about sexuality and the various pleasures to enhance it? If you need more information on basic sexuality—how to become aroused, how to have a satisfying sexual relationship—get a well-respected sex therapist's manual on sexuality. Libraries provide some books about basic information regarding sexuality, but very little about pleasurable expression. Sex shops or head shops do not offer the best information, and usually provide it in uncomfortable, sometimes dangerous surroundings. Sexuality boutiques, on the other hand, provide accurate information from basic sex education to information about massage oils and sex toys, to news about safe sex and the prevention of AIDS.

Unfortunately, I know of only five such quality, well-established boutiques in the country. To locate more such boutiques other than the ones I mentioned, your best bet is to ask a qualified marriage counselor or sex therapist in your area. These are the types of places marriage counselors or sex therapists will often send their patients to, so they might discover ways to enhance their sexual pleasure. And frequently, sexuality boutique owners will consult with sex therapists and have them conduct sexuality workshops or allow sex therapists to post their notices of sexuality workshops they are conducting. These particular boutiques are staffed by women who are used to helping people who feel embarrassed. The women are knowledgeable and there to help. The boutiques are clean, well-lit places, in nice areas of town.

GROWING SEXUALLY

"As long as we live, we are in the process of becoming something other than what we were," says Sally Wendkos Olds, author of *The Eternal Garden: Seasons of Our Sexuality.* [11] Allowing our sexuality to blossom and grow is as valid a growing process as any other. Whether you need to read more books specifically focusing on the mechanics of sex, or whether you need to talk to a sex therapist, keep reminding yourself that finding out more about "you," and ways to become the person you want to be, is perfectly all right.

At times, you may experience "sexual growing pains," as you tackle any past anger, fear, resentment or feelings of guilt, but you can then find relief and joy as you discover who you are as a sexual person. You don't have to box yourself into some sterotype that makes you miserable. And you don't have to continue to make excuses or feel your troubles are something you "just have to live with." You are never too old to explore and to discover your sexual self and share all that is uniquely "you" with your lover. May we all learn to accept better what is so much a part of us, and of being alive.

Points to Remember

1. The silly or hurtful notions we learned about sex can be unlearned, and replaced by more personally appropriate knowledge.

2. It is perfectly all right to talk about sex with your spouse, about your needs and desires, and to explore together the variety of ways to enhance your mutual sexual pleasure.

3. Accepting and expressing your sexual self is a valid growing process. When you make the effort to learn and grow, you help to prevent sexual boredom in your marriage, and stimulate sexual excitement.

9

For Better or for Worse?

How to Look and Feel Good for Yourself and Your Spouse

Jogging three times a week may not make you want to jog right into the woods with your spouse and "make love." Nor will it turn you into the sex god or goddess of the year, but an ever-increasing number of studies do indicate that exercise not only improves the quality of your life in general, but may also enhance the quality of your sex life.

> *"The pleasures of sex are not reserved only for long-limbed people who work out everyday. But they are enjoyed more by those people who have positive feelings about their own body and about their spouse's body."* [1]
> —Dr. Ruth K. Westheimer, sex therapist

Parents I have spoken to tell me that when they engage in some form of exercise, they feel much more positive about themselves and are able to cope better with the daily stresses of raising children, running a home and tackling the responsibilities of a career. Most importantly, they tell me they feel sexier, more like lovers, rather than some frumpy mom or dad for whom sex is merely an afterthought. Most parents related that they still have mostly weekend sex, but lovemaking is much more satisfying because they feel good about themselves. When they are feeling out of shape, it definitely affects their desire for sex, and the quality of sex. Studies conducted on exercise back up these feelings, though none are conclusive.

HOW BEING OUT OF SHAPE AFFECTS YOU SEXUALLY, AND WHAT YOU CAN DO ABOUT IT

"Exercise increases endorphins, the natural chemicals that make you feel good, but we don't know exactly how that affects sexual pleasure," says Los Angeles psychologist Linda DeVillers, who surveyed 8,500 women aerobic exercisers. Of the women she surveyed, eighty-three percent did some aerobic exercise three or more times a week, most for more than three months. Her findings indicated that: forty percent said their capacity to be sexually aroused had been enhanced; less than three percent felt less turned on; ninety-eight percent said working out lifted their overall self-confidence; eighty-nine percent reported a boost in sexual self-confidence; twenty-five percent reported an increase in sexual desire; and thirty-one percent related an increase in the number of times they made love. [2]

Sociologist Phillip Whitten of Bentley College in Waltham, Massachusetts, who studied self-image and sexual behavior patterns of one hundred and eighty male and female masters swimmers (those who participate in the USA Masters Program), from forty to eighty years old, discovered some interesting possible links between exercise and sex. These swimmers who worked out one hour a day, five times a week, had bodies that were in great shape. Whitten concluded that because of the swimmer's physical shape, other people may be more attracted to them. It was also reasoned that extensive exercise may boost testosterone, the male hormone, which may enhance sex drive, and that exercise improves the function of the heart and lungs, which helps keep people healthy so they can enjoy sex as they get older. Whitten pointed out that: ". . .the major factor is psychological. These people feel great about how their bodies look. They're confident enough to pursue sexual relationships." [3] He related that cycling, running or aerobics would produce similar results.

Having a good sex life is more than just a matter of finding the right time and place and having the adequate equipment. Good sex depends a lot on how you are feeling about yourself emotionally and physically. "Sexual health is tightly interwoven with total health: both depend on freedom from physical and emotional limitations," relate Masters and Johnson. [4] In fact, being in good physical shape,

---

MOTIVATING TIPS ON EXERCISING

♥ Choose an exercise or sport that you would really like to do. If you like to ride your bicycle, perhaps your husband can watch the kids in the morning, so you can ride your bike. Or if you like to walk or jog, find a time that will work for you. The idea is that if you pick a regimen you enjoy, your chances of sticking with your program are better.

♥ Work out with a friend. Form your own buddy system where you can encourage each other. This helps a great deal in your ability to stay motivated. If you are able to arrange for a baby sitter so you and your spouse can exercise together, this is even more ideal. One word of caution; if you have not done any exercise in several months or years, it might be a good idea to first see your doctor for a physical. You might even ask him or her about the best type of exercise for your age and ability.

♥ Do some warm-up stretching first, before you exercise, and some cool-down stretching movements afterwards, so you don't pull a muscle. You will be more enthusiastic about exercising or participating in a sport if you are not in pain.

♥ Try to exercise the same time every day. Schedule your time as you do your dates with your spouse, or activities for your children. *You deserve time to keep yourself healthy and happy.*

♥ Set goals for yourself, such as the number of pounds your want to lose or inches you want to take off your waist or hips. Keep a chart for yourself with short-term and long-term goals. Take your measurements once a week or every three weeks, and mark the pounds or inches lost on your chart. Reward yourself, not with food, but with something sexy and pretty to wear, such as new jogging shorts or a new tennis skirt.

---

experiencing a fitness that is right for you, may also help prevent what Masters and Johnson refer to as sexual burnout, a condition typically marked by a sense of physical depletion, emotional emptiness and a negative self-concept.

No matter what physical shape you are in, you can begin to do something about it right now. You don't have to look like a model or Mr. Atlas. You don't have to wait until the children get older. You don't have to wait for a vacation filled with outdoor activities. You don't have to wait until you stop feeling so tired. In fact, even if you are getting less sleep, once you begin to get some exercise, you will feel *less* tired. For example, if you are a full-time mom, you can begin by establishing a specific time when you take your baby for a long walk in his or her stroller. You get some exercise, and the baby gets to see lots of interesting sights. If it is raining or too cold, take your child to the mall and walk there.

Whether you spend your days at the office or at home, you can get up a little earlier in the morning and participate in a morning exercise program on television. Some mothers I know have to get up at five o'clock in the morning because this is the time their children wake up. They breast-feed their babies, then go back to sleep when their babies nod off again. But instead of going back to sleep, this is an excellent opportunity to tune into a yoga program, and try to exercise for twenty minutes. You will feel better, and still have a chance to catch a little more sleep. Nellie, a friend of mine who has three active boys under age seven, bought an exercise video tape that she especially liked, and began exercising for a half hour every morning while her children ate breakfast. Over the course of a year, she lost the fifty extra pounds she had put on over the years from her three pregnancies. My friend Jackie has her husband watch the children when they come home from work, so she can ride her bicycle for twenty minutes, three days a week. Still another friend of mine, Mary, takes a long walk everyday after she drops her kids off at school. Her husband Rob squeezes in jogging time before he goes to work in the morning. As a busy parent myself, I make time to do some stretching exercises between five-thirty and six o'clock in the morning, before my children wake up. My husband works out four times a week at the YMCA near his office.

I *know* it is no easier to fit exercise into your busy schedule, any more than it is to fit in sex, time for yourself or a vacation, but feeling crummy about yourself not only affects your overall well-being, but your sex life, too.

FIVE EASY EXERCISES TO GET YOU STARTED NOW

♥ *The Sit-Down Stretch:* Sit on the floor, with your legs out in front of you. Next, make a fist with each hand, and place one fist (knuckles facing forward) under each knee. Bend forward at the waist and stretch slowly. Do this about five times; exhaling upon exertion, inhaling upon relaxation.

♥ *The Deep-Knee Stretch:* Lay on your back on the floor, knees bent. Then, bring your right knee into your chest. Stretch. Next, do the same thing with your left knee. Stretch. Do each knee five times, alternating knees; exhaling upon exertion, inhaling upon relaxation.

♥ *The Tummy Trimmer:* Lay on your back, then prop your legs on a chair, so your feet and calves are resting on top of the chair; your knees and hips are parallel. Next, sit up and touch your hands to your knees; exhaling upon exertion, inhaling upon relaxation. Do this about fifteen times, gradually working up to thirty times, or even fifty times if you really want to help flatten your tummy.

♥ *The Stressed-Out Back Reliever Stretch:* Lay on your back again, with knees bent. Then push your stomach into the floor. Your stomach should be flat on the floor when you push, so you cannot get your hand under your back. Press for a count of five, then release; exhaling upon exertion, inhaling upon relaxation. Try this five times, working up to ten times or more, as you desire.

♥ *The Simple Push-Up:* Get on your hands and knees, bending your feet up so they don't touch the floor. Keep your back straight, tummy tucked in and arms parallel with your shoulders. Your hands should be facing forward, about ten inches out from the sides of your body. And your head should be parallel with your body. Then, slowly lower your chest by bending your arms; exhaling upon exertion, inhaling upon relaxation. Try to do five push-ups initially, working up to more push-ups as you desire.

In a study conducted by marriage therapist Richard B. Stuart and his wife Barbara Jacobson for their book, *Weight, Sex & Marriage: A Delicate Balance*, the authors made two surveys of approximately twenty-five thousand *Weight Watchers* magazine readers, most of whom were women. They discovered that by the thirteenth year of marriage, women had gained an average of 24.7 pounds. Their husbands gained an average of 19.4 pounds. Some women, it seemed, felt less attractive and were concerned about their weight. The men, on

---

MOTIVATING TIPS ON DIETING

- ♥ Do your food shopping by yourself *if you can*. Avoid taking your kids along who invariably pester their parents for candy, potato chips and soda—all the types of goodies you may want to avoid. One rule I have adopted with my children that helps to keep these tempting treats out of my house, is that they can have goodies on the weekend, not during the week, except if they have been invited to a birthday party or have a class party. After dinner, we have fruit for dessert. On the weekends, we have ice cream and I try to make it a festive occasion. We put little candies on top of our ice cream or make sundaes. This way, we avoid the extra sugar during the week, but have something to look forward to on the weekend.

- ♥ Ask your children to help you make their lunches. If they are older, they can make their own lunches, and you can avoid being near the food.

- ♥ Try using your children's smaller plates and serve yourself smaller portions to help you reduce your food intake.

- ♥ Take small bites and savor your food. When you tell your children to chew, chew, chew their food, try to remember this advice yourself.

- ♥ Have two appetizers, such as a salad and a small portion of pasta for your meal, when you go out for dinner, instead of having a filling entree. Waiters and waitresses are often very accommodating and will be glad to bring your salad first, then serve your other appetizer as a main meal. Many restaurants also now offer low-calorie entrees, which you may want to take advantage of.

---

the other hand, felt their added bulk meant that there was more of them to love.

In my interviews with parents, the wives felt less attractive as a result of their weight gain, and also felt less attracted to their husbands if their husbands had gained weight. The husbands were definitely concerned about their weight, but not as concerned about it as their wives were. In regard to their wives' weight, the husbands wished their wives were in better shape, but were not as concerned. What seemed to affect sex for parents the most, as far as physical aspects, were the wife's feelings about her own body, and about her husband's body.

"If I don't feel good about myself, then I just don't feel like anyone should feel good about me, especially my husband," said Denise, the mother of two sons, seven, and four months. "My husband likes sexy nighties and it's hard to get them to fit when you are overweight. They just don't look quite right on me and it does affect our sex life. If I don't feel sexy, then I don't think anyone should think of me as sexy."

Another mother of an eight-year-old daughter and a three-year-old son, felt the same way. "When I feel good about my body my whole attitude is so different," explains Cindy. "I can act sexy and cutesy. If I am feeling fat and ugly, that's how I act, and that's certainly not a turn-on. When I'm feeling cute and sexy, my sex drive is definitely stronger."

And still another mother of two sons, four and two revealed: "How I feel about my body depends on how bright I want the lights," quips Patti. "If I don't feel that great about my body, then I keep the light level down lower in our bedroom, and try to block out how I look."

It seems that spouses in fairly healthy marriages love each other no matter what, but they would like each other to look better. "I know I am turned on by a man who has a nicely shaped body. When I look at well-built men, I secretly wish my husband cared enough about his looks to get more physical exercise," related Katha, the mother of a three-year-old son and a newborn daughter.

A father of two teen-agers told me: "I love to watch my wife ride a bicycle when we are out riding alone together. Just seeing her doing something physical, being in the physical mode, rather than in a business mode, really turns me on."

And another father of three active young sons, who bought his wife a membership to a women's health club told me: "We used to make love in the dark; now we make love in the light," says Jason. "My wife Ruth is much less inhibited about her body now that she works out. After she exercises she just has this glow about her and that turns me on." When I spoke to Ruth, she told me what physically attracted her to Jason. "An outdoors kind of man really excites me. When Jason has been outdoors getting exercise, then comes home, he's energized and that really is a turn-on."

Exercise and diet, or using good nutrition sense, go together if you want to keep your body healthy and energetic. Any diet, preferably a well-balanced one, which has fewer calories than you expend and higher carbohydrates will cause you to lose weight. By combining good dieting sense with a good exercise program, you can shed the pounds you want to lose. Diet experts tell us that losing weight slowly is better for your health because you have a tendency to feel less tired, become anemic or incur other health problems for yourself. The key to losing weight is eating nutritious foods from all four food groups, reducing your portion size and increasing your energy expenditure through sensible exercise. Before you begin any diet, it might be wise to check with your doctor first.

What to Do When You Take Care of Yourself, but Your Spouse Doesn't

When both spouses exercised, the quality of sex for them seemed better. When one spouse exercised and the other spouse didn't, there was trouble in the bedroom. "Personally, how compatible two people are in bed has a lot to do with their physical fitness," says Roberta, owner of a women's health club in Dallas, and mother of an eight-year-old son. "My husband does not exercise and it definitely affects our sex life. He does not have as much energy as I do, so his sexual stamina is not as strong as mine." Roberta's husband, who is just over six feet tall, and weighed two hundred and twenty-five pounds when they married nine years ago, got down to one hundred and seventy-five pounds, but through the years his weight went back up again. "He didn't like how he looked and neither did I, so we sat down and had a long talk about it. I told him, 'Look, this just doesn't work for me. You are not attractive to me when you look like this, and it is important for you to be attractive to me.'" Roberta and her husband drew up a written agreement, basically stating that he would get down to a healthier weight. "I told him I didn't expect him to be one hundred and seventy-five pounds because realistically, he would have to starve himself to stay at that weight, but I did expect him to stay at around one hundred and ninety pounds, so we made a written agreement with each other: 'This is the weight you will stay at because that's important to me.'"

Most husbands and wives don't expect each other to be super thin or super muscular, just physically fit. For example, one mother told me: "When I'm around men who exercise and their wives don't, I definitely sense this kind of feeling like, 'I wish she would.' I'm sure it would probably make the wife more attractive to the husband. Even if she doesn't have a terrific figure, just the fact that she gets out and exercises, it seems, would make a difference."

Confronting the Endless Excuses

While we would all like to feel and look better, we seem quite adept at sabotaging our efforts with excuses. We pile up enough excuses to make ourselves immobile and sabotage not only ourselves, but our spouses and our sex lives. One mother I spoke to had told her construction worker husband: "You don't need to lift weights; you lift sheet rock all day!" Fortunately, the husband was wise enough to realize the importance of exercise and did find time to work out regularly at a gym.

Here are some common excuses and my suggested answers.

EXCUSE: "I've paid my dues."

For some couples, it seems that marriage is a license to relax and not to try to impress each other anymore, but this attitude could not be more damaging to a marriage. Part of the romance of our courtship was that we *did* try to impress each other, to look sexy. It was important then and it is just as important now, in order to keep our mates interested. Your spouse feels good, looking at you, and you feel good, looking at your spouse. A healthy marital love is unconditional, but it is also tempered with consideration.

"If you want your spouse to love your body, and if he wants you to love his, then you have to help each other take care of those bodies—not through crash-and-fail dieting, but through sensible eating and sensible exercise," urges Dr. Ruth. [5]

ANSWER: Realize that if you want your spouse to be excited by you—to be attracted to you—it is important to take care of yourself.

You will feel better, and your marriage will be stronger and more exciting. Talk to each other about looking attractive. Perhaps you can work together to design your own self-improvement plan. Again, be considerate of one another's feelings, and don't assess blame.

EXCUSE: "I'll never look like those gorgeous bodies in those magazines, so why try?"

This is another sabotage trick. If you keep comparing yourself to fashion models, you don't have to bother with exercise and diet. But instead of getting yourself off the hook, you are only repressing your feelings of frustration and perhaps low self-esteem. The only way to deal with them, is to face them.

In an extensive Gallup survey conducted for *American Health* magazine on body image (July/August 1988), researchers discovered that the thinness mania that gripped all of us in the 60s is giving way to a new appreciation for body type differences, the idea being that we each have a *unique physique*. Building the healthiest body you can have is the important factor, not whether you look like cover star Elle Macpherson or Arnold Schwarzenegger. In addition, another very important discovery was that, as far as physical appearance, men are less demanding of what they expect women to look like, and vice versa. *American Health* reports: "The average man and woman have bodies that are, well, average. He's 5'10" and 172 lb., with a 33" waist; she's 5'3-1/2" and 134 lb., and wears a size 10 or 12 dress... What's startling is that we seem to *like* being average. Women say they'd much rather have an average body type than a thin body type. What seems even more unbelievable is that, although women *think* men like them lean, a full 65 percent of men say the ideal woman has an average body type; only 18 percent think thin is heavenly...." [6]

As for what women expect of men, *American Health* says: "Women *do* say they prefer muscular men to lean ones, but they're not as demanding as men think. Men with medium-to-broad chests and shoulders—and at a run-of-the mill 5'11" and 171 lb.—are just fine with women." [7]

SUPPORTIVE WAYS TO HELP YOUR SPOUSE STAY HEALTHY

♥ Keep all fattening foods, such as potato chips, cookies and candy out of the house. If your spouse is craving an ice cream sundae or apple pie, offer to take him or her out for dessert on the weekend.

♥ Try to cook more non-fattening foods, such as fish and chicken, and season with just lemon and garlic powder, instead of salt and sauces. Make an effort to find six or seven healthy meals your spouse and kids will love. The old saying, "the way to a man's heart is through his stomach," may still be true, but you can do it with low-calorie meals that will also help save his or her heart.

♥ Serve more raw vegetables in the form of a salad, instead of cooked vegetables with butter and sauces.

♥ Serve fruit for dessert or low-calorie gelatin.

♥ Talk to your spouse about your feelings in a non-threatening way. Instead of saying, "Boy, you really have put on the pounds, lately;" a better approach might be to say: "You know, honey, you really have a handsome face. You would really look dynamite if you lost a few pounds. Can we talk about this?"

♥ Make up your own written contract of how many pounds your spouse should lose, if he or she is willing to try this. You might also make up your own chart, including various weight-loss goals.

♥ Sign yourselves up for dancing lessons, or make a date once a week to go bowling, if your spouse refuses to do exercise of any kind. Or, if you go bowling, you can pack your own low-calorie picnic, instead of munching on peanuts and candy at the bowling alley.

♥ Have a picnic dinner at the movies, and pack your own treats of diet soda, sandwiches, fruit and non-salted popcorn.

♥ Be as helpful as you can if your spouse is inclined to want to lose weight. Buy your spouse a special gift, such as sexy underwear or a nice shirt or blouse, when he or she does lose a few pounds. Keep the encouragement up, and celebrate when his or her goal weight is reached.

"We don't all have the same metabolism, so we can't all look like Nancy, for example, who is 5'6" and weighs 110 pounds," says Joyce Brown, owner of Élan, a women's health club in San Anselmo, California, who stresses fitness over thinness. "For someone who has a slower metabolism to try to look like Nancy, who may have been thin all her life, is not only unrealistic, but unhealthy. That person would have to starve herself to look that way."

Looking and feeling fit is the goal to strive for. If you have been defeating your efforts to exercise and eat properly because you felt you had to look model thin, you now have no excuse not to get started. In establishing realistic weight goals, again, it might be a good idea to talk with your doctor first. Remember, that it is best to lose weight slowly and eat a well-balanced diet. Eat smaller portions, and avoid "empty calories," those foods full of sugar or starch that provide no nutrition. Also discuss an exercise program with your doctor. Find out which type of exercise or sport would be most beneficial for you, personally.

EXCUSE: "We don't have sex very much anymore, so why bother to stay in shape?"

Staying overweight and not exercising is an excuse for not talking, and not talking is an excuse for staying overweight and not exercising. I'll explain. In some marriages, affection is not given, either because the couple's parents did not display affection, or for other reasons which has caused the couple's love for each other to erode or both. In some cases, when one or the other spouse craves affection, but does not receive it, nor talks to his or her spouse about it, there is a tendency, instead, to turn to food.

In their survey, Stuart and Jacobson discovered that: "The unsatisfied hunger for touch is mysteriously transformed into hunger for food... For the touch-deprived, only sweets hold that special magic normally found in a tender embrace. What vitamin pills offer to those who don't have adequate nutrition, sweets provide for the emotionally malnourished." [8]

This theory is not new, but what is interesting is that Stuart and Jacobson explain that when a woman's husband can't or won't have sex with her, she stifles her sexual desire by overeating. "Many women apparently believe it 'hurts less', if they deliberately contribute to their own rejection by gaining weight. It's as if they're saying,

'You can't fire me, I quit!'" relate Stuart and Jacobson. [9] No study I know of has been done regarding men's feelings about being sexually deprived. It may be that they bury themselves in their work, or, have an extramarital affair, rather than overeat. My point is that sabotaging your own body because you are afraid to discuss your emotional and physical needs is a tragic excuse for not being and staying fit.

ANSWER: Talk to each other. Seek professional help, if necessary.

Discussing your feelings is the key to breaking out of this trap. If you don't express your needs, your spouse will never know what those needs are. If you have expressed your needs, but your spouse seems unresponsive, try to find out why.

EXCUSE: "I am what I am. Why should I change?"

Some women and men have a fear of intimacy. Rather than discussing their fears and seeking counseling, if necessary, they hide behind their fat. They mutually inhibit each other. Jill Harkaway, assistant clinical professor of psychiatry at Tufts University and psychologist at New England Medical Center, Boston, agrees with Stuart and Jacobson that weight can be a way to avoid being sexually intimate in marriage. For some people, it may feel easier and safer to stay within the "maternal" or "paternal" ideal of what they feel parents should look like, than to break out of this mold and free themselves to be sexy and sensual.

ANSWER: You cannot repress your feelings or ignore them in the hope that they will just go away.

In order to get relief from your frustrations, fears, depression or anger, you must talk about your feelings and get them out in the open. Don't allow your fears to hold you captive in an overweight body. When you get your feelings out, then you have a chance to deal with the fear-of-intimacy issue and help yourself and your marriage.

EXCUSE: "Whenever I try to lose weight, my spouse buys fattening foods and seems to undermine my efforts, so why try?"

In some cases, when wives or husbands make an effort to lose weight, their spouses knowingly or unknowingly sabotage their efforts. Some husbands, for example, feel jealous and threatened if their wives lose weight because they fear if they do begin to look too attractive, they will stray. According to Stuart and Jacobson, wives complained that their husbands wouldn't change their diets or routines to adjust to their weight-loss program; some men refused to give up fattening foods or keep sweets out of the house. Other husbands wanted to help their wives, but were not sure how to do that or did not know what their wives expected of them.

> **ANSWER: If your husband is sabotaging your efforts to lose weight, talk to him about it. If your wife is undermining your efforts to look and feel good, talk to her about it.**

If you are the one trying to lose weight, you might write down your goals and expectations, then show your list to your spouse. *Spell it out* so your spouse clearly understands exactly what you are trying to achieve. You might make up another list for your spouse and call it, "Ways You Can Help Me Achieve My Goals." You might also have a family meeting if your children are old enough to understand, and discuss your goals and expectations with the whole family, so you can elicit everyone's support and cooperation.

Don't Worry, Be Sexy

In deciding to change the way we look and feel about ourselves, we can either continue to blame our troubles on forces that appear beyond our control and use that as another excuse, or we can take responsibility for ourselves and realize that we do have some freedom to make choices. We don't have to box ourselves into a stereotype that goes against the way we would really like to feel. Respectable parents have a right to look and feel like lovers. There is a romantic and sensual side in all of us waiting to come out.

Finding your romantic or sensual self means allowing a more confident, sexier human being to emerge through exercise, proper diet and anything else that makes you feel good, such as a vacation, getting a weekly manicure, updating your wardrobe or getting a massage. One smart mother of two young sons picked up on her

husband's interest in trying a massage and made him an appoint-
ment with a masseuse at his local health club. He enjoyed it so much
that he now gets a massage once a month. Another tuned-in mom
bought her husband a gift certificate to get a manicure.

Still another mom buys her husband sexy underwear, instead of
the usual, basic white. For some husbands, one of the biggest turn-
ons is to go with their wives to buy sexier, tailored clothes once the
wives had lost weight and had leaner figures to brag about. One wife
discarded her baggy sweat pants and sweat shirts in favor of a sexy
tennis outfit, which her husband loves. "When I am wearing my
tennis skirt it is much easier to keep in touch with my body and not
let my weight get out of control," related the wife.

UNCOVER YOUR SENSUAL SELF

♥ Think back to the days before you got married. What did you used
to do to make yourself feel attractive and sexy? As a woman, did
you wear makeup? As a man, did you wear cologne? Whatever you
did to help yourself feel sexy then, you can do again.

♥ Focus on some feature or quality that is attractive. Everyone has at
least one particularly appealing feature. If your hair is especially
thick and beautiful, don't hide it under a scarf. Buy some pretty
barrettes and accentuate this feature. If you have a handsome face,
take care of it. There are a lot of nice lotions on the market now just
for men. You don't have to look like a model to play up the
wonderful features you do have.

♥ Buy clothes that flatter your shape, whatever shape you have. Don't
hide your physique under bulky sweaters or oversized sweat pants.

♥ Learn to accept compliments from others. When someone pays
you a compliment, just say "thank you." Don't feel you have to
apologize or make excuses for the compliment.

♥ Keep telling yourself that you are a worthwhile person and you have
a right to look and feel good.

And a thirty-seven-year-old mother of two daughters, ten and seven, who began exercising for the first time ever, told me: "I lift weights at a local health club and when I walk out of that place I feel like I can do anything I put my mind to! I feel *very* good about myself. I have always been happy with my husband and kids, but I feel I have something extra now. And because I feel better, I do enjoy sex more."

When you take responsibility for your physical and emotional health, and devote more time to yourself, you are taking responsibility for your own sensual and sexual pleasure, as well. "As much as you might like to think that someone else will turn you on and give you joyful paroxysms of sexual pleasure, in actuality we are each responsible for our own eroticism," say Masters and Johnson.[10] No one is going to sweep you off your feet but you! No one is going to make you feel totally good about yourself but you! If you feel stiff and tense from a lack of exercise, find a good program for yourself that you will enjoy and stick with it. If you feel flabby, find a diet that you can live with, not one that will make you miserable and cause you to quit. If you can't stand your hair, go get a new cut that will flatter your face. If you are trying to lose weight, but every time you turn around some member of your family brings cookies and potato chips into the house, have a meeting and tell them how this makes you feel and elicit their cooperation. Remember, you have a right to take care of yourself, but *you* have to take the initiative!

Points to Remember

1. No matter what physical shape you are in, you can begin to exercise. It is a good idea to get a check-up first and ask your doctor for suggestions on the types of exercises that would be best for you. But get moving! You will feel less stiff and be able to think more clearly. You will gain physical stamina, which will make you feel less tired.

2. Choose an exercise or sport you enjoy. This will increase your chances of sticking with it. Schedule a time to exercise that works best for you. And set short-term and long-term goals for yourself, such as the number of pounds you want to lose, or the number of inches you want to take off your waist. Reward yourself when you accomplish your goals, but not with food. Buy a new pair of jogging shorts or a new tennis skirt. When choosing a diet, pick one that

offers good nutritional advice that has you lose weight slowly. Avoid quick weight-loss schemes that claim one hundred percent success, or push amphetamines to suppress appetite, which only have a temporary effect and may also cause unpleasant side effects.

3. A healthy marital love is unconditional, but it is also tempered with consideration. If you want your spouse to be excited by how you look and feel, and vice versa, then you have to take care of yourself. Your marriage will be stronger, and your sex life will be more exciting.

10
Getting Away

How to Find Paradise in Hotel Heaven

"The first time we went away, Kevin was an absolute wreck," recalled Bonnie, mother of a son, seventeen, from a previous marriage, and two daughters, Jessica, eight, and Rebecca, four. "Kevin and I just had Jessica with us then, and I was pregnant with Rebecca. It was July, and I made all the arrangements for our vacation and just told him. 'We are going!' He said, 'I can't go. I can't leave Jessica.' I said, 'Yes, you can. We are *going*!' Then he told me, 'We'll go for one night.' I said, 'Two nights.' He said, 'I *can't* do it!' I told him, 'Yes, you *can*! We are *going*! Jessica will be fine!'"

"We left on a Friday to go to a little New England inn. We arrived around dinner time, and Kevin called the baby sitter. When he hung up the telephone, he turned, looked at me and said: 'You were so right to do this! We need to get away. I'm so glad you made us do this!'"

"The art of love is largely the art of persistence." [1]
—Dr. Albert Einstein, physicist

Leaving children behind to go off and enjoy a wonderful vacation or even just an overnight stay, is not always easy for any parent, but a very important issue to consider. When you allow yourselves some extended time away to focus just on each other, you get the needed rest you deserve, plus a chance to renew your love. Whether you are fortunate enough to go off to a luxury hotel, or whether you have to scrimp and save to afford a moderate hotel room or a cabin somewhere, it doesn't matter. Any place where you both can have some peace and quiet and be lovers in an atmosphere of total privacy, can be your own slice of heaven.

Don't let feelings of guilt prevent you from getting away together. Granted, the precious years we have to be with our children go by so fast, but again, so do years we have to be with our spouse. I spoke with many couples about going away together. The majority were reluctant to go away and either had never gone anywhere, or had only taken a trip once or twice since their children were born. For some of these parents, this meant not having gone anywhere together for over nine years! Sadly, one of the couples I had interviewed, who had never taken a trip away together, I later learned were in a terrible car accident and the wife was killed, leaving two children under the age of eight. I am not telling you this to scare you, but just to suggest that none of us has any guarantees on life. When you give and give so much to your children, think about giving some time to yourselves.

ANSWERS TO EXCUSES FOR NOT GOING AWAY

Often, we are so busy worrying about our children, we forget to think about our own needs, especially when it comes to taking a weekend or longer amount of time away without kids. For parents who have never had a vacation *sans* kids, the very idea sends shivers down their spines.

One mother I spoke to, who has a five-year-old boy and a ten-month-old girl, told me that she and her husband had never had a vacation away, just the two of them. Her eyes showed a yearning for some extended time alone with her husband, but her unrealistic sense of duty kept dragging her down. She had her "guilt trips" honed to a science, and rattled off ten reasons why she couldn't leave her children.

If she could ever bring herself just to grab her husband and go away, I'm sure her kids would be fine in the hands of a competent baby sitter, and she and her husband could once again discover what attracted them to each other in the first place. Instead of dreaming

HOW TO DEFEAT PARENTAL GUILT AND OTHER ANXIETIES, SO YOU CAN TAKE YOUR VACATION

♥ Talk honestly about your feelings of guilt and your fears about leaving the kids. Discuss *all* your reasons for not wanting to go. By talking about your fears, you will put yourselves in a better position to deal with them.

♥ Discuss any anxieties that you may have about going away together. Often, couples who have not been away since their honeymoon, may have worries about being together. What would we talk about? What would we do? By talking openly, you can dispel a lot of these worries and begin to make plans for going away.

♥ Work together in your search to find someone to care for your children so you can get away. Often, there is a tendency to designate this as "the woman's job." But if the husband is involved as well, and this is looked upon as a "joint effort," this further helps to lessen anxieties and prevent resentments.

♥ Interview potential baby sitters together, so you are both satisfied with the person you choose.

♥ Plan your vacation together, once you have found "the right baby sitter." Talk about where you would like to go, and what each of you would like to do. This is a chance for the two of you to get away and you will want to do activities together. But also remember that this is a vacation for each of you to enjoy separate activities, as well. If you want to relax by the pool and read a book by yourself for part of the time, let your spouse know. By allowing yourselves a little "self time," it will increase your desire for "couple time."

♥ Realize that saying good-bye and driving away may be one of the most difficult things you will ever have to do. If it helps to talk about the children for the first hour, then do so. Otherwise, concentrate on the two of you. If you are both nervous and anxious about going off together, just accept the fact that this is part of the normal process of going away. It takes time to shift gears, to go from being parents to being a couple again. Before you know it, you will be laughing and joking and holding hands again, just like you did on your honeymoon.

about going away with each other, they can work together to find recommendations of baby sitters. They can interview baby sitters together so they both can be satisfied in finding a person they like. When they finally find someone, then they should make all the arrangements and preparations for their vacation together. This helps to dispel anxieties and resentments and is a good preparation for being a couple again for an extended amount of time.

"When I was growing up, parents in my hometown seemed never to leave their houses for longer than six hours, and they took that much time only for major events like weddings and wakes. Perhaps because of that, I find myself burdened with an overdeveloped sense of duty," relates writer Paula M. Siegel, in an article she wrote, "Bugging Out" for *Parenting* magazine. "I feel that I must be no more than five steps away from my son at night until he's at least old enough to be tried for crimes as an adult. Unfortunately, my husband Steve suffers from the same sense of responsibility, so there's no one around the house to whisper sly entreaties to lighten up." [2]

"Lighten up" is the key. Just as we must make a date each week to feel connected, we must also make a date to have some extended time away without the children—two weekends a year or a week, at least—to get really reacquainted and break free from the everyday hassles and stresses that can interfere with our being a couple. Don't allow your unrealistic sense of parental duty or your list of endless excuses keep you from making time to be a couple.

EXCUSE: "I can't find a baby sitter."

ANSWER: A good competent baby sitter can be found if you are willing to make the effort to find one.

Call baby-sitting agencies and talk to them about your specific needs. Sometimes, hunting for a good agency takes work, but it is worth it. If you have relatives living nearby, and with whom you would feel comfortable leaving your children, ask them if they would be willing to watch your kids for one night or for three nights. If they have kids, too, maybe you could trade baby-sitting services. You could also do this with friends or neighbors. To get recommendations for overnight baby sitters, ask members of your church or synagogue, your health club, parent support group or ask your child's teacher. Sometimes nursery or elementary school teachers are interested in baby-sitting for a weekend or for a week during the summer to earn extra cash. Ever since my oldest daughter was nine months old, my husband and I searched and found good, responsible baby sitters so that we could go away at least two times a year for a long weekend. At times, our search took a lot of effort, but having the opportunity to be a couple for an an extended amount of time made it all worthwhile.

EXCUSE: "No one can care for my children as as well as I can."

ANSWER: Perhaps this is true, but there are competent, bright people around who enjoy children and who have a great deal of experience with children.

In fact, our very first overnight baby sitter and the mother of two teen-agers, was very helpful in working with us to get our daughter to go to sleep at night without having to be rocked constantly. And while we may not like to admit it, sometimes our children need a break from us, and really enjoy having someone new to play with them and show them new games. Our current sitter is a great cook, and my kids love tasting all the goodies she makes for them when we are away, such as muffins with fried eggs and melted cheese inside, and her special lemon fish.

EXCUSE: "We can't afford it."

ANSWER: With the enormous financial stresses most parents must bear in order to provide for their families, I can certainly understand this one, but even if you must scrimp and save for months in order to afford one night in a hotel, as several couples I interviewed did, again, it is worth it.

In fact, if you can trade off with friends and neighbors, you may be able to work out a situation whereby your neighbors take your kids for one night, and you have your house to yourselves. Then you can do the same for them. This way, you incur no cost, and still have some extended time together. There are ways to work this one out, and cheaper in the long run than paying for marriage counseling sessions when one day you look at each other and wonder why you no longer feel close.

"Several years ago, my mother had been ill for a year and I had been taking care of her. Finally, my husband and I decided we had to go away because our marriage was falling apart," relates Jessie, mother of three children, ages five, nine and eleven. "So we finally got a baby sitter and went to Jamaica for a week. Unfortunately, I spent the whole time worrying about my children, so our vacation didn't turn out to be the great romantic, sexual adventure that we had hoped.

"When we came home, a week after our trip, I approached my youngest daughter as she was brushing her teeth with the new toothbrush her baby sitter had gotten for her and said: 'Boy, that was really a hard time for you when Mommy and Daddy were gone, wasn't it?' 'No,' she told me. 'We had the best time ever!' So, I thought there was a real lesson in that. I could have relaxed that whole week because she was certainly having fun.

"I guess the point is that sometimes, some of our fears are unfounded. There is this feeling that we have to give our children so much attention. We have to be so concerned about where they are and how they are doing, when really, they can function quite well under someone else's care."

We love our children and certainly wouldn't leave them with some looney who hates kids. As for other excuses, like finances, you can either invest some money in your relationship, or spend it later on marital counseling sessions or a divorce lawyer. Frankly, I believe it would be much more fun to spend it on a vacation with my spouse, even if it meant just an overnight stay in a pup tent. I am not saying you are bound for divorce court if you never take a vacation alone with your mate. But if you want to keep your relationship emotionally and physically close and exciting, it helps tremendously to have time to be a couple for more than just three or four hours during an evening out. "Going out for an evening is great, but it often feels like my wife and I are on a short chain," one father told me.

For parents who have never gone away without their children, or who would love to get away, but are still reluctant to do so, Eileen Shiff, M.S., director of the Child and Family Studies Program at Glendale Community College in Phoenix, Arizona, and editor of the book, *Experts Advise Parents* (Delacorte Press, 1987) offers this advice: "I think the thing to ask ourselves at a time when there are so many splintered marriages, is: What is one of the most important gifts we can give our children? The answer is a strong marriage. So if you feel guilty doing anything unless it is going to benefit the child, then think about taking a vacation in terms of strengthening your marriage. You are reconnecting with your spouse, and as a result, you are both going to come home renewed, refreshed and have more enthusiastic energy for the child, rather than resentful energy."

For parents who feel that no one else can take care of their children as well as they can, a good friend of mine who arranges at least four vacations a year with her husband, had this to say: "I know when your child is born, it is easy to feel that you are the only person who can take proper care of that child," explains Joy, mother of a six-year-old daughter. "But once that child is a little bit older, especially when he or she is in nursery school, if you can leave the child part of the day with a teacher, you can leave him or her with a baby sitter for an overnight stay or for a weekend. Another person may not care for your child exactly the same way, but it doesn't necessarily make the way the person is handling the situation, wrong. So what, if your baby sitter gives your child orange juice instead of apple juice, or let's her have a cookie before dinner. It is not going to be the end of the world. I think kids need a break from their parents, too. It makes it really nice when you do come back home, and both you and your child really appreciate the time you spend together."

If You Just Can't Stand the Thought of Leaving Your Children Behind

While I believe it is better to make some time to be away to focus on just the two of you, if this is not possible, for whatever reason, here are some ideas.

Now, more than ever, an increasing number of hotels, resorts and even cruise ships are catering to families in such a way that kids and parents have fun together, and also have fun while apart. Club Med now has over six "miniclub" resorts, which offer day camps and baby-sitting for kids two to eleven years old. It also has a "baby club,"—Sandpiper Bay resort near Stuart, Florida—that has already accommodated over two thousand infants. Some other hotels that offer day camp situations are: San Francisco's Four Seasons Cliff Hotel; Lake Arrowhead Hilton Lodge, in the mountains seventy-five miles east of Los Angeles; most of the Sheraton hotels in Hawaii, as well as two in San Diego—the Sheraton on Harbor Island and the Sheraton Grand. The Hyatt Regency in Washington D.C. runs a summer program for kids, from ages four to twelve where parents can drop their children off at four o'clock in the afternoon, and pick them up as late as midnight. Cruise lines also offer programs for children. Florida-based Premier Cruise Lines, for example, staffs its ships with youth counselors who supervise activities for kids from ages two to seventeen. They also offer baby-sitting until midnight after these programs are over. For more information, contact your travel agent, or write to: TWYCH (Travel with Your Children), an organization founded by mother and ex-travel agent Dorothy Jordon, that offers news on any type of travel you can imagine: 80 Eighth Avenue, New York, New York 10011, (212) 206-0688.

The decision to go away for a weekend or a week is a big step for many parents. For some parents, it is an agonizing one, but once you have made it, marked a date on your calendar and proceeded with your plans to find a competent baby sitter, you are over the hump.

In deciding when to take a vacation away without the children, don't wait too long. "You have to start when the kids are little, so they get used to you going, otherwise, you may get a lot of resentment from them when you do leave," says Kathy, mother of an eleven-year-old son and a thirteen-year-old daughter. Kathy and her husband have always taken two weekend trips and one week-long vacation per year. "Our kids have just accepted the fact that we go away," explains Kathy. "They don't have a choice, really. We give our kids a lot of our time doing things with them, including taking family vacations, so I don't feel guilty taking time off for my husband and me."

Problems do crop up, however, when the children do get older and want to come, too, and the parents feel reluctant to leave them home. They no longer have to worry that their children are going to drop food all over the floor and drive the waitress crazy at a restaurant, so it's easy to give in. If you have been used to taking vacations with your spouse, but now feel that maybe your teen-agers should come, too, resist the urge.

I would like to point out that taking a vacation with your spouse does not preclude taking a vacation with your children. Family vacations are a wonderful way to stay connected as a family. It is nice to just enjoy fun times with your children without daily pressures. However, it is vital to get some time away as a couple, to be able to focus solely on each other.

One way parents of older children have gotten around this situation is to go on vacation during the two or three weeks their children are at camp. One mother I know, sends her two children, nine and fourteen, to her parents' home in another state. The kids love to visit their grandparents. And during this time, she and her husband have a vacation. For two weeks out of the summer they go away. During some summers, however, they have spent their vacation time at home, and visited local sights they hadn't had a chance to see, or tried restaurants they hadn't had a chance to try. The bottom line is to make time for yourselves, however you can manage it.

ROMANTIC WEEKEND GETAWAY IDEAS

- ♥ Stay at a bed and breakfast in Napa Valley, California, and tour the wineries together.

- ♥ Walk hand-in-hand through fall leaves and make love in front of a cozy fire at a New England inn.

- ♥ Swim together in a cool pool during the hot summer at a quiet motel.

- ♥ Ride horses through deep green woods, then sip drinks by a stream next to your lodge.

- ♥ Watch the snow fall from your cabin window.

- ♥ Lie on a beautiful beach near a lake or the ocean; know that any time you want to, you can run back to your hotel and make love and not have to be quiet so the kids don't hear you.

- ♥ Explore art galleries, museums or other cultural events in your favorite city.

- ♥ Find a quiet spot for your favorite activity—whether it's skiing, hiking or biking—and be sure to bring along a packed picnic for a romantic break.

Preparing the Children

In order to help ensure a good time on your vacation, it is essential that your children be left with a baby sitter who is familiar to them and in familiar surroundings, preferably in their own home. Your children are less apt to miss you if they remain in the environment they are used to, and within their everyday schedules doing what

---

A CHECKLIST FOR LEAVING YOUR CHILDREN WITH A BABY SITTER

♥ Schedule play dates or dinner dates for your children with friends before you leave. Let your baby sitter know of these plans, and give her the names and telephone numbers of the friends and their parents.

♥ Make a list of activity suggestions for your baby sitter that she can do with your children while you are gone. Also, discuss any ideas your baby sitter might have regarding activities.

♥ Talk to your children openly about your vacation; where you are going, what activities you might be doing, whether it is swimming or hiking. Talk to them about the activities they would like to do with their baby sitter while you are gone.

♥ Ask your children about any favorite foods they would like to have while you are gone, either a snack they could get themselves, or some meal the baby sitter could fix for them.

♥ Don't forget to leave those extra goodies that will help your children deal with missing you, for example: a photo of the two of you; a tape recording of your voice reading your child's favorite bedtime story; a love note for him or her to open after you have left; a little present he or she can open for each day you are gone, such as a box of crayons, a can of modeling clay or a new book; and perhaps stickers for a small child, so he or she can put a sticker on each day that you are gone, and get a better idea of when you will be home.

♥ Make sure you help your child choose any appropriate gift or party clothes needed for any events he or she will attend while you are gone (for example, a friend's birthday party).

---

they normally do when you are home. However, if you have arranged for them to stay with a familiar relative or neighbor in whose home they feel comfortable, that's fine, too. In addition to making sure they feel content with their caretaker and surroundings, it is important that you help your children to feel that while you are away, they are going to have a special time, too.

"What we tend to do is feel like we are betraying our children by going, so we don't talk about our trip," says Shiff. "We feel guilty about it and that creates tension in the home. It is much more helpful to say to your children, 'We are all going to have a vacation. Mom and Dad are going to the mountains, and you are going to stay with Grandma, or whoever is coming, and have specific, fun activities to do.' That way, everybody gets involved in the excitement of what they are going to be doing."

To make the getting away process as easy as possible, parents I have interviewed often like to draw up lists of their children's schedules, foods they like to eat, friends they like to play with and activities they like to do, to give to the baby sitter. One mother lays out her children's clothes for every day of the week that she and her husband are to be gone. Parents also like to leave photos of themselves, tape recordings of their voices reading their child's favorite bedtime stories, little gifts and even notes on their child's pillow telling him or her how much they are loved. Parents arrange play dates and dinner dates for their children with friends ahead of time, as well. Whatever makes it easier for you to leave on your vacation is fine. The better you feel about leaving your children, the better your chances of having a wonderful vacation.

One important reminder: When you plan activities that are going to cost money, such as going out for pizza or going to the movies, be sure to leave your baby sitter some cash. The parents I talked to usually leave some entertainment money in an envelope. It is also a good idea to set some money aside for gasoline if your baby sitter is going to be driving your children to various events. And leaving some cash "for emergencies only" is never a bad idea.

Important telephone numbers, instructions and specific rules are also set up, especially in regard to calling home. "The kids or baby sitter never calls us, unless it is an emergency," relates Tina, mother of a six-year-old girl and nine-year-old boy. "We rarely call if we are away for a weekend, and only call once a week if we are gone for a longer time. This seems to work out pretty well. Since we are very comfortable with the people we leave our children with, we really have no worries." One mother told me that only her husband makes the call home because if she calls, her children start complaining about who hit whom, and which kid took the other kid's baseball or doll away.

Still another mother rarely calls home if she goes away for a weekend. She finds her children get homesick and cry on the telephone. "It used to take me a good hour to relax again after one of these tearful conversations, which didn't do me or my children any good," says Patti. "I had to keep reminding myself that they have been diverted by our baby sitter and are doing something fun."

If you have not worked out a satisfying system for preparing your children so you can both have a good time while apart, it might be a good idea to sit down with your spouse and decide what your rules are going to be, and what specific instructions and important telephone numbers you want to leave. You might each have different opinions on how frquently to call home, how much information is vital to give your baby sitter and so forth. In setting up your system, don't forget to leave room for some flexibility.

"I tell my baby sitter who comes for the weekend, these are the rules that cannot be changed, and these are the rules that can have an exception," relates Connie, mother of two boys, two and four-and-a-half. "I tell my sitter I want this to be a special time for her and the boys, so these are the rules you can bend. The idea is that 'Mom doesn't let us have popcorn in the family room, but Suzy did.'"

Sometimes, kids get sick, as we all know. If your child gets sick the day you are planning to depart for the vacation you have so carefully planned for, don't panic and cancel your trip. Calm down and assess the situation. Sometimes when children are sick and their parents are not around, they can get frightened, but if your child is not terribly ill and feels comfortable with your baby sitter, there is no reason not to go away. If your child does become ill with the flu, or if he just has a cold, but you feel you would be spending the whole trip agonizing over the situation, then you must use your best judgement.

If you cancel, however, you and your husband must immediately pick another vacation date on your calendar. Just knowing another date is established can make such a cancellation bearable. Try not to get discouraged, and don't give up.

"THE GREAT ESCAPE"

Every year, around Valentine's Day, my husband and I go away for a weekend. I usually set the mood by sending him one of these giant, five-foot-high by seven-foot-wide telegrams. It comes in a ten-inch by twenty-inch envelope, and when opened, takes up one wall of his office. I usually say something like: "You'll always be my hunk!" His co-workers enviously walk by, make a point to peek in and ask, 'What did Anne do *this* time?!' They all know me there. My husband reciprocates with something equally crazy and romantic.

One time, I brought our children into the city to have lunch with Daddy. After our wonderful family time, we drove to our hotel, showed the kids where Mom and Dad would be staying, then *he* took the kids back home with him and met our baby sitter at our house. My husband went over the final arrangements with her, then met me back at our hotel. The idea was that I could have a chance to rest, and not poop out after my first glass of champagne. It worked, and we had a great Valentine's Day celebration! My point is that just as you prepare sexually and mentally for a date night, you can also do the

---

SPECIAL TREATS TO BRING ON YOUR ROMANTIC GETAWAY

- ♥ your own aromatic potions, such as bubble bath soaps, massage oils, lotions or scented candles
- ♥ sexy lingerie
- ♥ a tape recorder and your own collection of soft music tapes "to make love by"
- ♥ any gourmet foods or wines that you particularly like
- ♥ sexy poetry you may want to read to each other
- ♥ any favorite books you have been wanting to read, so you can each have some relax time on your own
- ♥ a collection of sexy love notes you can put in obvious places around your hotel room, to create your own romantic environment and get the ball rolling

same for your vacation. By setting the stage for romance, you are more likely to increase your chances of getting romance.

One couple I spoke to always buys a variety of bubble bath soaps to take with them because they love to take bubble baths together. "We each go on separate shopping trips and then surprise each other when we get into our hotel room," related the wife. One mother I spoke to always brings sexy lingerie: "All those skimpy things I can't wear at home." And still another couple fills a cooler with all their favorite gourmet foods. "We buy special goodies and surprise each other," says Mary, the mother of two young sons. "I know my husband Craig loves these certain olives, and he knows I like a particular wine."

Still another couple brings oils so she and her husband can give each other a body massage. In planning your trip, you can each set the mood by either doing something romantic or thoughtful, or by bringing something to make your vacation, *your* vacation. Bring a book of poems, a tape recorder and tapes so you can play your own romantic songs, some scented candles or a bottle of champagne. If you want passion, you have to create the conditions for passion!

HAVE FUN WITHOUT REALLY TRYING

This is your vacation, second honeymoon or whatever you want to call it, so relax and don't expect to have sex twenty-four hours a day unless you really want to. Having sex is high on many parents' agenda when they do get away, but many couples also related that they love to sleep, talk, read a novel alone, engage in a sport or just sit still.

"One time, we checked into a hotel and watched some dumb television show for two hours straight, in the middle of the afternoon," recalls Becky, mother of three-year-old twin girls. "I thought, 'Oh, great, we are paying eighty-five dollars a night to sit here and watch this stupid T.V.,' but that's just what we needed in order to wind down."

Katie, a mother of three boys, nine, six and a-year-and-a-half, has found that the first day of the vacation is always a bit difficult. "Jim and I spend so much time apart on a daily basis, that when we suddenly have all this time to spend together, it takes some getting used to," she says. "We both understand it, and don't put too much weight into it. We might be a bit cross with each other for the first few hours, then later we reflect and laugh. We know it isn't anything, then the vacation is fine, but it happens on almost every vacation."

The important thing to remember is not to expect too much from each other, and to give each other space. Try not to plan a lot of activities. If you have a specific activity you want to do, and your spouse doesn't, you may have to compromise. It is also all right to engage in a sport or other activity separately. Each of us needs some self time, in addition to couple time. "In order for Jim to relax, he becomes more athletic, so I will encourage him to play a game of tennis or volleyball," says Katie. "And I will be very content to have some quiet time to read a book, or take a boat ride on a lake."

"I look forward to taking a two-hour, uninterrupted bath, or going for a long walk on the beach by myself," relates Linda, mother of two teen-agers. "It's really important for me to have that time, and for my husband to have time to himself. In order to build closeness, there's got to be that sense of separateness, too."

"I love to go out jogging on the beach or sit in the hotel coffee shop and read my newspaper if Bill wants to sleep late in the morning," says Janna, mother of a daughter, five, and son, eight. "We understand each other's need for self time and don't try to play 'program director' with each other's time."

When couples come together, they seem to do a lot of talking, laughing and gradually settle into a sexual rhythm. "A lot of times we have sex in the morning, and sex at night. If we have been out playing during the day, we come back to our hotel, take a shower together, nap and then make love," says Dawn, mother of a seven-year-old daughter and four-year-old son. "When we leave the kids, house and stress behind us, it's as though we've stepped off the merry-go-round and been set adrift on a quiet sea. . ."

"Having some time just to relax once or twice a year or more, is like getting a vitamin B shot for your marriage," one mother told me. "It is nice to be able to shift gears." Often, however, even a brief vacation isn't quite enough to ease all the stress parents must deal with in a given year. To help ease some of the stress, I'd like to encourage couples to try Dr. Debora Philip's *Intimacy Island* technique, which I mention in chapter 6. It is one way to get away mentally, When you can't physically. Another way to get away without leaving home, is plan to take off a vacation day when your children are in school if they are older. You and your husband can have a great time playing hooky from work! Or, if you have a neighbor, friend or baby sitter who is willing to watch your child for the day, meet your husband at his office for lunch and take the afternoon off together. Or better yet, go out for breakfast and spend the whole day together. You will feel like you have had a nice "mini-vacation," without leaving town.

When parents make the time to go away together, a wonderful thing happens. They become lovers. They hold hands and take long walks in the woods, make love in front of a cozy fire, have breakfast in bed and enjoy many of the things they used to enjoy before they had kids. Sometimes, they act like kids themselves. "One weekend we went away to this quaint bed and breakfast place in the mountains. It had snowed, and everywhere it was white and beautiful. It was the kind of inn where there was a fire always crackling, and smells of home baked bread and muffins tempted you endlessly," remembers Lisa, the mother of two small boys. "On the last morning of our visit, we went crazy and ordered everything on the breakfast menu, which a kind old lady brought to our room, with fresh linens. We stuffed our faces, and have laughed about that morning for a long time."

The main reason parents make a point to go away is not just to obtain relief from the stress of raising children, or to cure the "hornies," although this is a big part of it. They go away, I believe, to recapture the passionate essence of the love they know is hidden deep within their hearts somewhere, the reason that prompted them to get married in the first place. So don't be afraid to let the passion of your love come out. Be persistent in keeping it alive, by getting away together.

Points to Remember

1. Make a vacation date. Find a competent baby sitter who will watch your children overnight or for a long weekend, so you can have some extended time to focus on being lovers. Don't allow excuses to get in your way. You *can* find responsible baby sitters. If a lack of money is an issue, trade off baby-sitting services with your neighbors, friends or relatives. If your neighbors are willing to watch your children at their house, then you can turn your own

home into a motel. In the long run, finding a way to be together is a lot cheaper than spending your money on marriage counseling sessions, when one day you look at each other and wonder why you no longer feel close.

2. It may be hard for you to leave your children to go away on a vacation, but one of the most important gifts you can give your kids is a strong marriage. When you go away with your spouse, you are helping to keep your marriage strong.

3. When you have finally managed to plan your vacation, don't forget to pack special treats, such as sexy lingerie, bubble bath soaps or seductive poetry. Give each other some self time initially, to unwind and change gears from being parents to being individuals. Then, allow yourselves time to just enjoy being a couple. Discover all over again, the love you share—without those many interruptions.

11

"I Need a Break!"

How to Get Some "Self Time"

During my high school years, when my fellow student friends and I were playing "ace reporters" for our school newspaper, I sometimes used to disappear into the storage room, which I claimed as "my office," to compose my deepest thoughts. Naturally, I became the subject of a lot of jokes. During our farewell journalism banquet in the spring of my senior year, my friends jokingly, lovingly, presented me with a huge poster on which they had carefully scrolled these words from Henry David Thoreau: "I love to be alone. I never found the companion that was so companionable as solitude." [1]

I took the poster home, hung it on my bedroom wall, and I treasured those words as I prepared to go to college. Now that I am married and have children, I am more grateful than I ever thought I would be for those moments I am able to grab for myself. I adore my husband and kids, and value the times I am with them, but let's face it, we all need time for ourselves, and I don't mean just five minutes of peace and quiet in the bathroom! Some parents don't even get *that*, and feel compelled finally to let the little buggers in, when they have heard, "Mommy, what are you *doing* in there?" one too many times. Wanting to have some time by yourself is not a silly or selfish notion. It is another way to nurture yourself and recharge your "parent batteries" and your "lover batteries."

*"I just wanted to have brunch at a quiet restaurant by myself.
My kids thought I had a fight with my husband; and my
husband kept urging me to take a girlfriend along so I wouldn't
be lonely. I finally made it to the restaurant with my newspaper and was far from lonely. I was thrilled!"*
                              —Barbara, a mother of three children,
                                   twelve, eight and five

For a married person with kids, it is especially difficult to go from
being a mom or a dad to being "a lover," if you have not taken some
time out to just be "you." As parents, we have such a great lack of
privacy, that even our very thoughts or daydreams are interrupted
by children who always need something, need help with something
or just want to tell us about Johnny's new pet frog or Janet's new
stereo system. "I used to think I was going crazy because I was always
losing my train of thought mid-sentence, then I realized it was
because my kids were always interrupting me!" related Karen,
mother of two young sons.

Parents need self time to collect their thoughts, to feel like individuals first, before they can feel like lovers, or even the loving
parents they want to be. In fact, mental health experts nationwide

---

WHY WANTING TIME BY YOURSELF IS GOOD FOR YOU

- ♥ You will be a calmer, more loving person when you have had a chance to be good to yourself.

- ♥ You will have more patience to deal with problems that come up with your spouse and kids.

- ♥ You will be less resentful when your spouse says he or she needs some self time.

- ♥ You will have a chance to think and focus on situations involving yourself, your spouse or your children, and you will be more productive in dealing with them.

- ♥ You will have an opportunity to concentrate on some of your own personal goals, and decide the best course of action toward achieving them.

are now telling us that solitary time is essential to the well-being of the parent and to the health of the family. Parents who allow themselves some self time reduce stress, increase their creativity and feel less resentful when other people place demands on them.

Ironically, sometimes having less togetherness actually enhances marriages. According to Dr. Douglas Sprenkle, director for the Doctoral Program in Marriage and Family Therapy at Purdue University: "Couples are less critical and irritable after each mate has had some time to do something he or she enjoys. They are also more willing to listen to each other and to compromise because they don't feel overwhelmed or used." [2]

> *"Once upon a time there was a little fish who was a bird from the waist up and who was madly in love with a little bird who was a fish from the waist up. So the fish-bird kept saying to the bird-fish: 'Oh, why were we created so that we can never live together? You in the wind and I in the wave. What a pity for both of us!' And the bird-fish would answer: 'No, what luck for both of us. This way we'll always be in love because we'll always be separated.'"* [3]
>
> —Vassilis Vassilikos, Greek novelist and poet,
> elucidating the theory "Absence makes
> the heart grow fonder."

SELF TIME: THE VITAMIN PILL FOR LOVERS

Parents I have spoken to from all around the country and from various economic backgrounds, felt very much the same in regard to having or not having some private time for themselves. When they had some time to themselves to think, dream or relax, they felt less anxious, less stressed out, more in control and better able to deal with the demands of life. They appreciated their spouses and children more, and felt that having some self-nurturing time actually improved their relationships with their spouses and children. From a sexual standpoint, they felt better about lovemaking. In other words, the resentment spouses often feel when they do not get some self time, which can interfere with sexual desire, was less of an issue.

"Having some time to myself definitely gives me a new perspective on life at home," related the mother of a three-and-a-half-year-old son. "It makes me more willing to listen to my husband's problems. It affects our relationship in a positive way because I get a new burst of energy." Another mother of a two-and-a-half-year-old daughter felt the same way: "Having a little solitude helps my self-esteem, which helps me to feel better about lovemaking, about my life and about my relationship with my husband." Still another mother of a seven-year-old daughter and ten-year-old son told me: "I pampered myself last week. I got a facial, manicure, massage, the works! My husband said, 'Go ahead. It's your day. Enjoy!' It was great! I felt refreshed and liberated!"

Fathers, too, need some time off, and those who did take it, felt better about themselves, their wives and their children. "I feel grate-

---

WONDERFUL WAYS TO GIVE YOUR SPOUSE SOME SELF TIME

- ♥ Plan ahead. Ask your mate on Wednesday, what he or she would like to do on the weekend, as far as having self time. If he wants to play golf on Saturday morning, then you watch the kids. On Saturday afternoon, perhaps he can watch the children so you can do something on your own.

- ♥ Try to be empathetic to your spouse's need for self time, and don't give your husband or wife the third degree for wanting to go to a restaurant or movie alone.

- ♥ Try to be patient and understanding. Equal amounts of self time on a given weekend may not always be a fifty-fifty proposition. Some weekends you may get more self time. Other weekends your spouse may get more.

- ♥ Arrange to have a baby sitter on a Saturday morning, then you both can go your separate ways, and have time alone.

- ♥ Protect your spouse from the children, telephone calls and neighbors dropping by, if he or she is having some time alone at home. Then, your partner can do the same for you.

- ♥ Recognize your husband's need to go "out with the boys" or your wife's need to spend time with some girlfriends. Don't try to make your spouse feel silly or guilty. There is nothing wrong with getting together with friends separately, once in a while.

---

ful that my wife will baby-sit so I can play golf. Having the time off makes me feel less anxious and stressed out. It also makes me appreciate my wife more," the father of two children, nine and seven, told me. "When I have had some solitude I feel I am able to be more giving and understanding towards my wife and children," an obstetrician and father of three adolescent daughters related. And still another father who takes time for himself and watches his children so his wife can have time off, too, explained: "Life is too short not to allow yourself a little freedom. I'd rather come home and have everybody be happy, than have the floor always be spotless."

Solitude is a vital element of any love relationship. If we deprive ourselves of it, I believe not only the marriage suffers, but the family unit as a whole suffers, too. "When too much time goes by without time for myself, I get grumpy and resentful. I keep hostility all pent up inside myself, then become a real witch," said the mother of a three-year-old son.

Another mother of a six-year-old daughter and four-year-old son said: "Not taking time for myself makes life very stressful for me, resulting in poor relationships at home with my spouse and children." And another mother of five-year-old twins, a son and a daughter, explained: "When I don't take time for me, I feel resentful and less able to look at situations realistically or objectively. I also feel jealous of the time my husband spends relaxing. This has caused many an argument in our household."

Today, we lead such busy life styles that even a bubble bath seems like an unattainable luxury, but the good feelings that can come from giving ourselves little gifts of time, will benefit our marriages, and make us feel more like lovers. "Getting in touch with one's own center rejuvenates marital relationships," adds Sprenkle.

Why It Is So Hard for Us to Take a Break

For centuries, women have been socially conditioned to take care of other people. In the past, if a woman, especially a mother, sat down to read a newspaper, watch television or pursue some hobby, she was regarded as a poor mother or neglectful spouse. For dads, on the other hand, it has always been more socially acceptable for them to engage in some relaxing activity. Times are changing, but old beliefs die hard. Instead of spouses finding time to relax, or helping each other find time to relax, both moms and dads are running themselves ragged and feeling guilty that they aren't doing enough for their children. This is especially true of dual-career parents who pick the kids up at day care, open their front door and hit the home turf running. Meyer Friedman, M.D., and Ray H. Rosenman, M.D., authors of *Type A Behavior and Your Heart*, refer to this habitual sense of time urgency as "hurry sickness," and relate that it is ". . .the most significant trait of the Type A man or the Type A woman." [4]

Hurry sickness or the "modern disease," as they call it, carries over into the bedroom, too. A great joke from American humor illustrates the point:

> *"What does the French woman say when she is made love to?"*
> "Oooo, la, la!"

> *"What does the Italian woman say when she is made love to?"*
> "Mama mia!"

> *"What does the American woman say when she is made love to?"*
> "Frank, the ceiling needs painting!"

It is almost as if we need permission to allow ourselves to take a break. But no one is going to come along, put his or her arm around your shoulder and say, "Boy, you look beat. Why don't you take a break?" Only *you* can mentally take yourself by the hand and lead yourself to a quiet place.

The feeling that we always have to be doing something—makes me wonder where we left our priorities. Granted, your children need you and you certainly cannot ignore their needs. However, you cannot ignore your own needs, either.

As we move through the nineties, I fear more and more of us will be suffering from what Dr. Georgia Witkin-Lanoil refers to as "role multiplication." She explains that men today are experiencing "role confusion," while women are experiencing "role multiplication," which means that women's roles are not changing; they are piling up. Women today expect themselves to be "Super Mom," i.e. fill their roles as wife, mother and job-holder simultaneously, and do them all on a full-time basis, says Witkin-Lanoil. "She uses herself as cheap

---

PLEASANT WAYS TO TAKE AN UNEXPECTED BREAK

♥ Drop your children off at school, head for the nearest coffee shop with your newspaper and spend an hour on yourself.

♥ Avoid spending your lunch hour, at work, running errands. Go out with friends or spend a relaxing lunch hour by yourself.

♥ Buy that novel you have always wanted to get, and when your baby is napping, read it. Forget about washing the clothes. Spend one, two or three hours a week enjoying yourself.

♥ Take a break from your morning duties. If you are usually up before everyone else, making coffee and getting breakfast ready, give yourself a morning off. Set up the coffee maker, put out cereal bowls, make the orange juice the night before, so you can spend those few precious morning moments on yourself.

♥ Make the time spent riding the train, bus or ferry home from work each night your personal time. Instead of working on that financial report, grab a soda and read the newspaper or catch up on those letters you've been meaning to send to friends.

♥ Enjoy a free moment to yourself, once you have finally put the children to bed. Refrain from rushing to clean up the kitchen or doing laundry. Take a half hour to relax in the bathtub or give yourself a manicure.

♥ Take a morning aerobics class to give you that burst of energy and vitality to help you start your day.

---

labor, adding more and more roles as the years go by. Soon she no longer has time for herself." [5]

Men are suffering from "role multiplication," as well. The minute they are pronounced "Father," they know they must also add to their roles of "husband," and "provider," the role of "all-encompassing nurturer," because if they *don't*, someone is going to be left holding the dirty diapers and it isn't going to be Mom. Of course, Mom is within earshot, stirring up a gourmet dinner because her neighbor down the street is doing that, too!

We are becoming a highly competitive society, so competitive that we are competing even with ourselves, and don't dare step off the merry-go-round for fear we will lose our "super human" status. "If I'm not working, I feel I should be with my family. That's the primary reason I never take time for myself," says John, the father of two daughters, eight and ten, and a son, six.

Mike, the father of a two-year-old son told me: "I have a few minutes to myself to unwind when I come home from work, but that's about it. Sometimes, I wish I just had another apartment I could go to—some place where I could just sit and do what I want." Other fathers I spoke to related feeling guilty about taking time off for themselves, so they rarely did, or if they allowed themselves a break, felt guilty the whole time they were taking it.

Many mothers I spoke to felt equally guilty grabbing any time for themselves, and some moms were wearing their martyrdom like a badge. "I didn't take any time for myself until my third child was born," said Sandra, whose children are now ages ten, eight and four.

Ellen, the mother of a seven-year-old girl and two-year-old boy, told me: "I don't know if it's a martyr syndrome or not, but I feel like this is my place right now, being Mom, and putting everyone else before me." Several weeks later, when I spoke with Ellen again, she related that it was beneficial for her son and herself, for her son to be in preschool playing with friends while she spent time on herself. "I always felt I didn't approve of preschool if it wasn't necessary, but for my own sanity, it really is. My son enjoys it! *He* didn't cry when I left him there. *I* did!"

ROLE MULTIPLICATION: THE MANY HATS WE WEAR AS "SUPER PARENTS"

- ♥ *Super Moms' Hats*: nurse, maid, referee, taxi driver, class party mom, pizza day mom, nursery school aid, pet keeper/pet finder, cook, laundress, seamstress, Girl Scout leader, etc.

- ♥ *Super Dads' Hats*: Saturday taxi driver to the fast food place, little league coach, part-time toy finder and fixer, part-time pet finder, gardener, cook, maid, Boy Scout leader, etc.

What happens is we brainwash ourselves into thinking we really shouldn't take some time for ourselves, and even condition our families into thinking like this also. If and when we do take some time for ourselves, our spouse and children have been so conditioned to seeing us *not* taking time off, that they resent it when we do, thereby recycling the guilt. "When I went away for the first time ten years ago to spend a weekend by myself at a health spa, my daughter Johanna was two years old," related Michele. "You wouldn't think a two-year-old would remember, but she still says to me, 'Do you remember when you went away and Daddy made us eat hot dogs two nights in a row?' She still doesn't like me to go away, even though I only go one weekend a year."

On the flip side, however, a mother of a thirteen-year-old daughter and eight-year-old son, who has gone away by herself for one weekend a year for the past several years, told me: "My kids don't mind when I leave. They realize it makes me feel better, and they like having the whole weekend with their dad."

Our children will survive. Our spouse will survive. And we will all be happier allowing ourselves some time off. We certainly don't want our children to grow up to be martyrs. In nurturing ourselves, we are in a sense nurturing them, by being good role models.

How to Be Good to Yourself

If you want to make some changes in your life so you and your spouse get some individual private time, you have to make the change yourself. No one can do it for you, not your spouse or your children. Things may be a bit rocky at first as you and your partner work out a schedule for self time, and as your children adjust to the idea that Mommy and Daddy need some solitude, too. But in the long run, everyone will be happier. "You can never estimate the needs of children until you have them, and the amount of time they require is enormous," explained Walt, the father of a four-year-old son and one-year-old daughter.

"I love being with my children, but you have to have some time away, otherwise, they just drive you nuts. You start to yell at them over little things that you wouldn't yell at them for if you weren't on edge. I just came to the conclusion that you have to make your own time. You can't feel guilty about taking it, or worry that your kids are going to be with the baby sitter for an hour."

You are in charge of your life, not your children, not your spouse. You have to decide what your needs for solitude are, and verbalize them to your partner. "Freedom lies in being bold," Robert Frost once said.[6] So stop making excuses for wanting time to be "you."

Treat Yourself Right

Teach your children to do more for themselves.

A three-year-old can learn how to dress himself or herself, and make a bed. A five-year-old can help set the table for dinner and feed the dog. A ten-year-old can sweep the floor and help wash the dishes. A teenager can learn to iron his or her clothes. One busy mother of six children, has her four oldest kids make their own lunches for school. Another mother I know sets out cereal bowls, spoons, cereal and pours milk in a little pitcher every Friday night, so her two daughters, four and six, can get their own breakfast on Saturday morning. You will not only be boosting your children's self-confidence by allowing them to be more independent, but you will free yourself up so that you can create the time that you need.

Teach your spouse how to help.

Both moms and dads are prone to the martyr syndrome. Women, however, are especially vulnerable and often will wait to be rescued. They are afraid to ask for help, and will wait until their husbands or children notice how exhausted they are and tell them to take a break. The problem is their husbands or children are usually so wrapped up in what they are doing that they may not notice. Relates Dr. Witkin-Lanoil: "Mothers who wait to be rescued by others become disappointed, angry and stressed: disappointed because any rescue that does come will probably not be well timed; angry because they have given a great deal of power to others; stressed because they must continually show the world that they need rescuing."[7] Another problem is that husbands and wives are not sure how to give each other a break. Once you have gotten up the courage to make your needs known, you must tell your spouse when and how you want to take your break. You have to be specific. A good example might be for you to say to your spouse: "I'd like to have two hours of time by myself at home. Could you please take the children to their gymnastics class on Saturday morning, so I can have that time?"

Plan your escape.

Parents I have spoken to find it very helpful to plan some self time, which is usually on the weekend, in advance. They talk on a Wednesday or Thursday night about their needs for private time on Saturday or Sunday. Some parents have even worked out schedules weeks or months ahead of time. Still other parents have a regular system organized so there is no question who gets out of the house on which nights. "It's almost standard that the weekend before Father's Day, my husband goes camping by himself," related Rhonda, mother of three teen-agers. "I usually take one weekend a year for myself and hole up in a nice hotel with my diary and trashy novels." Another mother worked out a system whereby every other Sunday she gets to stay in bed, while her husband fixes breakfast for the kids and plays games with them. On the other Sundays, it's his turn to stay in bed. "I usually wander out of the bedroom around ten-thirty in the morning," said Marcia, who has a twelve-year-old son and nine-year-old daughter. "I often don't sleep that late. I just read the newspaper or daydream, things I never used to let myself do." Still another couple gives each other one night during the week where they can each go out with their friends. She goes out with her girlfriends, and he goes out with the guys. "As much as we love each other, we feel it is important to maintain other friendships," explained Gloria, mother of two sons, ages five and three.

Hire help.

Often, teen-agers who may not be available to baby-sit on a Friday or Saturday night because they have dates, may be available to sit during the day on a Saturday or Sunday. If you decide to go this route, you may not only be able to get some self time, but also time together as a couple after you have had your solitude. Your moments together as lovers become even more rewarding because you have each been able to feel rejuvenated at the same time.

Play.

When you do get some private time, spend it on yourself, doing something you enjoy, not trying to catch up on laundry or washing the car. Take yourself out to breakfast, go to a movie, get a massage or manicure or spend all morning browsing through a bookstore, but allow yourself to have fun.

The Value of a Night Out with the Boys or the Girls

Frequently, there may be subjects you like to discuss that your husband couldn't care less about, and vice versa. When a woman has a chance to talk with other women friends, it gives her an additional emotional outlet. And when a man has a chance to talk with other men, it gives him an additional emotional outlet. Just as we cannot be everything to every child every minute, neither can our spouse always provide for all our emotional needs. Nurturing and maintaining friendships gives us the space that every marriage requires.

"I have my famous duck room that I can come to each evening if I need time alone," says Howland, father of a six-year-old daughter. "I can surround myself with the things that I like. My wife doesn't necessarily share my enthusiasm for the things that I like, such as my guns and fishing rods, but she has given me leeway to decorate my room however I want, even though she flinched when I hung the stuffed bird on the wall. No matter how much you love someone, you need time for yourself."

Pursue Your Dreams

In discussing the idea of having self time to relax, I felt it was vitally important also to include a discussion about having individual time to work on achieving personal goals. One evening, I was talking to a father about having his son come over to play with my younger daughter. As we were trying to organize a suitable play date, I mentioned to him that I was writing a book for parents. Aching with a need to talk to someone, he suddenly started telling me about the marital difficulties he and his wife were having because they were both unhappy with the job paths they had chosen. Instead of trying to find solutions, they were seething beneath a blanket of resentment, each blaming the other for not being able to pursue their original dreams. In the course of the conversation, he told me that when he and his wife met, he was on his way to medical school and his wife was about to join a professional ballet company. They were very much in love at the time, decided to get married and had their first child right away. Their dreams and goals went by the wayside. They had a second child and pursued other careers. I'm sure there is more to their marital difficulties and current separation than just lost dreams, but it made me wonder just how many husbands and wives

---

HOW TO DISCOVER AND PURSUE YOUR GOALS

♥ Make up your own wish list and title it something like: "What I would do and be if I could." Write down everything that comes to mind. Don't worry if it sounds crazy or wild, just let your imagination wander.

♥ Next, go down all the items on your list and consider those items that might be possible, or that you could realistically come close to pursuing. For example, if you always wanted to be an artist, perhaps you could take art lessons when the children are in school, on a Saturday morning or in the evening one day a week. If you always wanted to have your own business making children's hair accessories, for example, use your self time to find out how to go about doing this, how much it would cost to start it and to whom you would sell these accessories.

♥ Work on a written proposal. Write down all the reasons for wanting to pursue your dream and show them to your spouse. He or she may be more willing to listen than you think, especially if you have some solid facts and figures on hand. Don't back down and start feeling guilty. If you feel passionate about your dream, don't let it go by the wayside. Indulge your imagination. It's *your* self time. Then talk to your spouse.

---

are having trouble right now because they are not giving each other self time to grow? How many husbands and wives are not even allowing themselves to think about what they would really like to do, for fear of being ridiculed, misunderstood or ignored?

Granted, marriage is a compromise and it is not possible to fulfill some dreams due to financial or other situations, but you owe it to yourselves and your relationship to talk about them. Robin, a mother in her mid-forties, who has four children, ranging in age from eight to nineteen, told me her story: "One evening, we were talking and my husband, who is a CPA, told me that he always wanted to own his own firm. He works at a university and still has his certificate. Anyway, I just couldn't imagine starting over at our age, just scraping by on $16,000 a year because of the money we would have to invest in his business. We struggled and struggled with this idea. Finally, I just threw up my hands and said, 'All right, we have a fabulous retirement plan, take out forty or fifty thousand, buy a practice and go for it!' When I confronted him with it, he stopped and thought about it long and hard and said, 'No, I really don't want to work really hard for the next fifteen or twenty years of my life.' But we faced his dream. I think you have to be supportive."

Susan, a mother of two young daughters, whose dream was to stay home and write magazine articles, instead of being a full-time magazine editor, got her wish and was able to give up her job. She and her husband had extensive discussions about her dream and decided she could do it. "There are occasional days when my husband isn't totally happy with a specific task he has to do at his office, but he told me it always makes him feel good knowing I am home doing what I love to do," related Susan.

One father I interviewed was so tired living in the "rat race," that when he got some time to himself, he headed for the library to read about Mexico. Whenever he had some free time, he talked to travel agents. When he finally spoke to his wife about it, she was intrigued. Together they found a villa, put their furniture in storage and took themselves and their baby daughter to live in an area they considered to be paradise. The father, who is a professional photographer, supported the family with his photography and by being a tour guide for visitors staying at the villa complex where they lived. "I took care of those villas around us that were rented, and when tourists came who didn't speak Spanish, I acted as translator," said Robert.

This couple went down to Mexico with the intention of staying two months, and ended up staying two years. When I commented that it must have taken a lot of courage to do what they did, they admitted their dream took a lot of discussion and thought. "It was not easy for me to open myself up to the idea—to unlock," revealed his wife Andrea. "But Robert has the ability to unlock my locks."

Sometimes dreams work out. Sometimes they don't. But when you put your dreams on the table and listen to each other with empathy and understanding, you expand your capacity to grow as lovers.

Whether you use your self time just to relax, or to think about your dreams and how to pursue them, this is a healthy pursuit in itself. All of us need time alone, if for no other reason than just to sit quietly.

Points to Remember

1. It is not silly or selfish to want to have some time by yourself. Taking time off to nurture yourself, whether to read the newspaper or browse through a bookstore, is a good way to recharge your "parent batteries," and your "lover batteries."

2. Help each other to get some self time. Plan ahead. For example, you might say to your spouse on Wednesday evening: "I would really like to catch up on some sleep Saturday morning. Would you take the kids to soccer practice, then I will watch them in the afternoon."

3. Solitude is an important element in any love relationship. We all need some quiet time alone to think, to dream and to pursue goals. *You* have to make your needs known to your spouse and your children, however. So talk to them. Don't wait to be rescued.

12
Partners in Love

Building a Lasting Relationship

Loving someone is a struggle sometimes. It is indeed a great risk, because in loving another person we risk pain. Not to love—never to commit to all the hard work that loving someone entails—however, is to risk not living and discovering the more meaningful joys that can be found within a relationship.

> *"If someone is determined to not risk pain, then such a person must do without many things: having children, getting married, the ecstasy of sex, the hope of ambition, friendship—all that makes life alive, meaningful and significant."* [1]
> —Scott M. Peck, M.D., psychotherapist

In my many interviews with parents, I asked them what factors sustained them as a loving couple and kept their relationship strong. I also asked them if they had any rituals or traditions that they felt enhanced their life together. In all the stories and insights I have compiled, three vital elements—courage, commitment and communication—were a big part of their lives. These elements helped to make these parents strong, happy lovers, and better enabled them to raise strong, happy children. Because they had established, and are continuing to work to maintain a strong base as lovers, the result is a strong family base, too. A big benefit of sustaining these three elements, of course, is a loving and fulfilling sexual life.

It takes courage to risk loving someone because we have to be brave enough to be vulnerable. And yes, it is scary. But the rewards that can be gained by building a stronger love far outweigh the temporary fears we may feel.

So often, when something is bothering us, we are afraid to say anything to our spouse because we either don't want to hurt our husband's or wife's feelings, or we believe that somehow revealing our true feelings will "disturb the relationship." But, when you use the "I" word, instead of the accusatory "you" word, and tell your spouse how you *really feel*, you help to diffuse a lot of hidden anger, resentment or frustration, that if *not* diffused, will eventually come out in hurtful ways. When spouses try to keep their anger repressed, they may not only say or do things that are hurtful to each other, but hurtful to their children.

Telling our lover how we really feel about something is hard work for most of us because we have to push through our fears and the harmful messages we were given as children that "sad or angry feelings are bad feelings, and you don't talk about your bad feelings"; or as one mother constantly heard growing up, "Don't air your dirty laundry!"

These messages are so ingrained that they are hard to dump. But you must gather your courage and realize that when you talk to your partner, you *strengthen your marriage!* You are not tearing down anything or disturbing your relationship as long as you *communicate your feelings in a loving way*, and keep in mind that you are *building a relationship!*

When my husband and I met and fell in love, I was eighteen and he was nineteen. We may have had the carefree, "head-in-the-clouds" attitude of "being in love" some nineteen-odd years ago, but we were also fortunate enough to realize that we were "building a relationship," and we have been building it ever since. Anything of value takes work, and I honestly cannot think of anything more valuable than a strong, happy marriage and family. So when you get the nervous jitters, and start to back down when it comes to wanting to talk to your spouse, just remember that every time you push through your fears and talk to each other, you add one more block to your foundation as a couple and a family! You also build strength to help you deal with the struggles and crises that come your way.

A STORY OF COURAGE

Paul, who is a successful lawyer, a happily married man and devoted father of a four-year-old daughter, was just thirty-three years old when it happened. "I awoke late on a Sunday morning and went downstairs to get a cup of coffee," he remembered. "My wife had taken our daughter for a drive to see the autumn leaves. Suddenly, I found myself doubled over and lying on the floor from intense pain, trying to get to the telephone to call for paramedics."

Paul was rushed to the hospital, and doctors finally discovered, after thorough analysis, that he had diverticulitis, an inflammation of a sac-like pouch that had formed and was localized in the colon. Within a very short time, Paul's condition grew from severe to life-threatening. "He was so badly infected that doctors had to perform a colostomy, an operation that opens a channel between the colon and the skin and creates a new pathway for excreting bodily fluids. He was put on heavy doses of antibiotics before they could even make plans to go in and remove the part of his colon that was causing the problem," explained his wife Maureen.

Paul survived, but his ordeal was not over. He had to live with a colostomy bag for a year. During this year he went through three surgeries, yet continued to clerk in a law firm when he was able, and pushed himself through law school even when it meant listening to taped law lectures from his hospital bed. His wife continued to work full time, often rushing to visit him in the hospital after work during the weeks when he was there. She also cared for their daughter most of the time, who was then, only one. Paul and Maureen's relationship was severely tested, particularly their sex life.

"Neither one of us gets scared very easily, but this was something in our life that we never counted on," said Maureen. "We had always discussed what we would do if something happened to our daughter, or if something happened to our income, but you never think that something could happen to your spouse. At one point, I had to seriously think about what life would be like without Paul."

Doctors recommended that Paul and Maureen see a marriage counselor regarding the difficulty of dealing with Paul's colostomy, but they declined. Says Maureen: "We talked about sex, and decided we could handle this situation on our own. Paul was still the same person that I had always loved, and although the colostomy was difficult to deal with, we felt our sex life shouldn't stop just because we had something like this happen to us."

Paul wore a T-shirt so the colostomy bag would be less offensive to Maureen, and they were able to keep their sexual relationship alive. "I don't know what those twelve months would have been like, not being able to make love with each other," she related. "It just would have added stress to the whole situation. I'm not trying to sound like a saint, but we both looked at this situation as something we were involved in together. We were going to manage somehow."

Paul and Maureen did manage. In fact, together they were able to tackle a major life crisis and turn it into something positive because they loved each other despite their fears. Together they found strength.

Sex is important in a marriage. It is a way to love, to ease stress, to have fun just for the sake of having fun. To be a bit trite, it is the "icing on the cake." But if the cake is not strong enough, the icing slides off. In this chapter, I will discuss the three key elements—courage, commitment and communication—that can help keep your marriage strong, and your sex life satisfying. I will also discuss how adding special traditions or rituals to your life can enhance your relationship, by giving you a sense of continuity.

COURAGE AND COMMITMENT

"We've been through some pretty hard times, including a child dying, which was a whole growth process for us, but I've always felt, through all our pain, that my husband Jason is the one person I can be the most vulnerable with," explained Pam, mother of four children. "I can tell Jason anything and know he won't turn it into a club. We have a tremendous trust for one another. No matter how angry we get sometimes, we've always believed that we would find a path through the anger. You have to trust your spouse and this means not putting yourself first every time, which is hard."

Says Pam's husband: "We have a willingness to do whatever is necessary to make the relationship work. We have a strong belief that it *will* work!"

Trust and faith take courage and commitment. Together, these elements can make a powerful bond. In order to have them in your marriage, you must be willing to "let go" of your fears and not allow them to interfere with your desire and ability to work out whatever crises or difficulties are thrown in your path. It is also not only a matter of finding ways to work out difficulties, but in addition, finding some beliefs and methods of your own that will help you to strengthen your marriage and family.

"We really believe in monogamy. We believe in each other and in the family as a unit," stressed Christina, the mother of a seven-year-old daughter and five-year-old son. "We not only love each other deeply, my husband and I, but we really *like* each other. We are good friends. There was one point in our lives where our relationship did start to falter, but we took some personal growth seminars together, which helped us to learn more about who we are as a couple. The seminars helped us to grow and understand each other better."

Related Christina's husband, Don: "We are religious. We don't go to church every Sunday, but we keep strong by praying together. Eighty percent of the time we pray together as a family before we eat dinner. I stress saying prayers more often when we've had a really good day and I want to thank God for it, or when we are going through some difficult times."

"My parents have a wonderful marriage and will soon celebrate their fifty-year wedding anniversary, so their relationship has been a guide for me," said Carly, mother of three children. "When I married my husband, I made a commitment to stay with him until death do us part. We've been through some pretty rough emotional times together, including his extramarital affair, but we weathered the storm and came out stronger."

"We believe in the value of our relationship," explains Peter, father of two sons. "Building a good relationship takes a lot of work, but it is worth it. All relationships go through difficult stages, and other people may look more attractive during these times, but the same stages would occur with another person, too. You just have to care enough to keep trying."

"I basically believe that when you love someone you have to give 150 percent all of the time," emphasized Trevor, father of a two-and-a-half-year-old daughter. "Both partners have to be committed to each other for a loving relationship to be sustained. No matter how hectic our schedules are, my wife and I always sit and talk with each other in the evenings, after our daughter has gone to sleep."

"I am totally committed to my wife and family," related David, father of three young sons. "I will do anything to have our relationship succeed."

When I was a new mother and struggling to learn how to be a more patient, loving wife and mother, I was convinced that there was some mom out there in the world who was perfect. She always served

---

SUGGESTIONS TO GIVE YOU STRENGTH

♥ Set aside some time either each evening, twice a week or once a week to discuss your deep-down, gut-level feelings about your relationship; where the problem areas are and ways to improve the situations. If it is helpful, and your spouse is willing to participate, you can each make a list of the problems and solutions on a separate piece of paper. On the left side of the paper, write down some problem areas. On the right side, write down your solutions to each problem. Then, compare notes. In order for this time not to turn into a battle, you must both be willing to be open and empathetic on each problem and each solution.

♥ Consider marriage counseling as *a way to maintain your marriage.* Be willing to seek professional advice, if you become stuck on finding a solution to a problem, and the problem seems to be getting worse.

♥ Find a way to communicate spiritually. If you and your spouse are religious, set aside a few minutes each day where you can hold hands and quietly pray together. You can also do this with your children. If you are not religious, you can still set aside a few minutes each day, join hands and discuss all the good things you like about your spouse and your marriage and your family. Again, you can hold hands as a family, too, and talk about the wonderful things you share together, i.e. laughter, hugs, stories and special memories.

♥ Consider taking some marriage growth seminars together. Just as you might go to a cooking class to learn to make more delicious meals, you can go to a class on "communication in marriage," to learn to make a better relationship.

♥ Incorporate a sense of humor in your life. No matter how awful your problems appear, they will seem much more bearable if you can incorporate this positive element into your relationship.

---

gourmet dinners. Her children were always spotless after hours of play. And her husband was always ready to sweep her into his arms because she always looked so gorgeous. I carried around this image in my head and always felt like a failure because I could never measure up to this stereotype. When I finally realized that this image was really some hyped-up media myth, I felt better. I had a shot at becoming the loving mother and wife I wanted to be *on my own terms*!

In reality, there is no perfect wife. There is no perfect husband. There is no perfect parent. There is no perfect couple. There is no perfect marriage. There is no perfect family. There is only a lot of work, but a chance for the two of you to create the kind of life you want for yourselves. Having courage and a sense of commitment gives you the opportunity to make your marriage and family life what you want it to be, and can help you to deal with the rough spots that every couple encounters.

COMMUNICATION

Throughout the book, I have mentioned again and again the importance of talking to each other about your feelings. The other part of this message, which is equally vital is the importance of *listening to each other*. If you have ever really concentrated hard on what someone is saying to you, you will realize how much work this takes. Most of us only half listen or pretend to listen to what our spouse is telling us. Half listening has also been referred to as "selective listening," where we just hear what we want to hear, not always what our partner is saying and feeling and thinking.

> *"All communication in an intimate relationship is built upon mutual trust. To confide in another is to be relatively sure. . . that a ground of confidence is shared. Mutual trust grows as each partner takes the other into account as a person whose happiness is bound up with his own."* [2]
> —Dwight H. Small, author of *After You've Said I Do*

Being lovers means that you must each shoulder the effort and discipline of talking and listening. Anything of value takes work to maintain it. More marriages die of neglect than anything else says Dr. Alan Loy McGinnis. For couples who have learned this art of active loving, the results have been immensely gratifying. They discover things about each other that they didn't know before, increase their capacity to understand each other better or just reassure each other how much they care.

"One of the most intimate aspects of marriage to me is this sense that you understand each other," says Liz, mother of two teen-agers. "You know who your spouse is and you just love him so much. Or, when he knows you so well that he is one step ahead of you in realizing what you like sexually. This just comes from a lot of talking and listening. There are days when I come home from work after a hell of a day, and my husband has made me a cup of tea. This sounds so corny, but it's *this* kind of thing that turns me on! I don't expect my husband to read my mind all the time, but many times he just has an awareness of my needs. And it is not a matter of bringing home a dozen roses, as it is *him knowing me*! Sometimes I tell him something and he can repeat back to me the feeling that I am *really feeling*, but can't quite bring out right away. It's just that he's *there*, in the present, *listening to what I am saying!*"

Attention

There are few greater gifts in this life than giving someone your attention. In doing this, you are saying "I care about you!" Few people would disagree with me when I say that giving the gift of "attention," can mean much more than a dozen roses or a piece of jewelry.

By giving your spouse your full attention when he or she talks, you are much more likely to stimulate communication in your marriage, particularly if you have a partner who is not much of a talker. If communication is a problem to begin with, being brave and talking about it can help solve it.

"My husband wasn't real talkative when I first met him," recalled Arlene, mother of two young boys. "When I first started dating him I thought to myself, 'I could never get serious about this guy. It's too hard. He just doesn't talk enough.' But for some reason we kept going out and I realized it was leading to something more, so I thought, 'All right. I'm an education major. I took communication classes. It's time to teach this guy some communication skills, about paraphrasing and active listening.'

"He was real receptive, so we identified the fact that, first, we loved each other, and second, that we wanted to work on this. Now, he's a much better talker and listener. There are those days when I'll say, 'I don't think you're listening.' And he will say, 'Yes, I am. I am still listening even though I don't paraphrase everything you say or nod constantly.' He is a much more open person now. His whole family has noticed the difference."

Be persistent on this issue, but don't nag. Rather, express your feelings, using the "I" word. For example, you might say: "I really want to feel closer to you. Can you try to tell me what you are feeling?" *Not*, "You never talk to me."

"Moving from New York City to Washington, D.C. was an extremely stressful time for me," recalled Sandy, mother of two young daughters. "My father was recuperating from a major heart attack, and we were renovating this old house. One time, I had come home and found my husband and his brother had been breaking through cement and bricks, trying to open up this old fireplace. I took one look at the mess, sat down on the steps and cried and cried. I told Martin, 'This looks like how I feel right now, just all torn up!' And he understood, because we have always made an effort to talk about our feelings, instead of carrying them around inside ourselves."

Psychologists tell us that when we keep our feelings bottled up, they only eat away at us and make us angrier, more frustrated or

---

BE A BETTER LISTENER

- ♥ Give your spouse your full attention when he or she talks to you.

- ♥ Make eye contact.

- ♥ Listen with empathy. Don't lecture or criticize or try to solve your spouse's problem. Just try to understand, and acknowledge your partner's feelings by repeating the idea of what he or she is saying. For example, if your spouse says: "I felt so tired today that when the kids began fighting I just blew up and spanked both of them!" You might say: "You sound angry. It must have made you mad that the children weren't getting along, especially when you felt so tired." Often, just taking the time to understand fully what your partner is feeling, can ease tensions and draw you closer.

---

more depressed. These feelings have to go somewhere, or they become worse, frequently jeopardizing our health in the form of high blood pressure, stroke or heart attack. When you tell your feelings, you find relief.

"My husband was engaged once before and I was married once before. Those relationships were very difficult ones for both of us," revealed Jan, mother of two children, a girl, fifteen, and boy, twelve. "We realized how quickly one little thing can end a relationship, just because you don't talk about it. The problem gets totally blown out of proportion, until it drives a major wedge between you. Ryan and I always talk about problems before they become big deals."

Adds Jan's husband: "If something is bothering me I *know* it is important to tell Jan, even when talking is not that easy."

Talking is just as hard as listening sometimes. For some parents, talking about feelings is even harder because, as children, their own parents may not have listened or made an effort to understand. If you have grown up with the idea that you do not have a right to express your feelings, or that what you are feeling is not very important, learning to express yourself will take more work.

HELP YOUR SPOUSE TO TALK

♥ Make your spouse realize that you are willing to discuss any problems. If you notice that your partner is upset you might say: "You seem angry about something." This gives you an opening and a chance for your spouse to speak.

♥ Remind your spouse that the expression of his or her feelings is important. When your spouse says, "Oh, it's nothing," it is time for you to be more empathetic and say; "I care about whatever it is that is upsetting you. How you are feeling and what you are feeling is important to me because I care about you."

♥ Don't lecture, criticize or try to solve the problem right away. Once your spouse senses that you do care and seems willing to open up, give him or her your full attention and listen.

Even then, you can say to your partner: "It is scary for me to talk about what is bothering me, but I would like to learn how." If your spouse is understanding and patient, you can work on the communication difficulties together.

Listening, talking and caring stimulate the intimacy and trust that everyone wants in a marriage. As I mentioned before, if you want to have a satisfying *physical* connection, you must first establish a satisfying *emotional* connection. You can create and maintain good communications by listening with patience and understanding, and by making the effort to talk about needs, wants or aggravations, instead of keeping them bottled up inside.

Rituals that Carry On the Love

While courage, commitment and communication are the pillars of a strong marriage, including a happy sex life, rituals cement your commitment to each other. They add a sense of fun and continuity—a feeling that a loving life goes on even when difficulties or crises appear to threaten the love we have so carefully cultivated. Parents had lots of good ideas, and made me feel that despite ominous divorce statistics, there are many mothers and fathers out there who are having fun, and strengthening their love by incorporating rituals into their lives.

> *"Rituals and gestures are terribly important in the sustaining of love, and the reason they count for so much is that they have a cumulative effect. If you are married to a person who has been thinking up little favors and small gestures of affection for years, that becomes a mortar that holds your relationship together when the crises come and rattle your marriage."* [3]
> —Dr. Alan Loy McGinnis, marriage and family therapist

"We always celebrate the day we met as an extra wedding anniversary," said Robin, mother of three small children. "We will send each other cards or call each other, or maybe give each other flowers or a present. There's always some acknowledgment. This year, we met for lunch. We also made a little ceremony out of dinner together. We each had a glass of wine and clinked glasses. Also, usually every evening in the wintertime, after the kids go to bed, we sit by a cozy fire and talk."

ESTABLISH YOUR OWN RITUALS
AND ENHANCE YOUR RELATIONSHIP

♥ Create a ritual that will help you to communicate better with your spouse. For example, write a special love note to your partner once a week that includes all the positive aspects you like about him or her, and your relationship.

♥ Share a glass of champagne, a dessert or a particularly enticing meal every Friday, to celebrate the end of the week and the beginning of some weekend time together.

♥ Find an enjoyable activity you can do together once a week, such as going out to dinner, taking in a movie, playing a game of tennis or going on a walk.

♥ Make one night each week a "no television" evening. Play a board game together after the children go to bed, or just sit still with your coffee and listen to music.

♥ Spend one evening each week doing something wonderful for each other. Give one another a massage or wash each other's hair, or take turns reading some poetry if you enjoy good literature.

"Every year, on the night of our wedding anniversary, I get out the negligee I wore on our honeymoon," revealed Carol, mother of three teen-agers. "I only wear it once a year. It's just fun to do."

"Jack and I play this little game called 'Let's Make a Date,'" explained Mona, mother of two sons, seven and five. "I'll call him at the office and say, 'Hi, Jack, I was wondering if you could come over Friday night for dinner.' Then he will say, 'I'll have to get back to you.' Then he will call me a few days later and say, 'Friday night is fine. What time?' I'll tell him a specific time, then he will come home Friday night bringing me flowers and I'll fix a special dinner. Our kids think this is great!"

Couples who took the time to create and carry on their own personal rituals reported that these rituals brought them closer, and helped to ease the stress in their lives. Here are some stories parents told me, regarding the various rituals they celebrate:

"My wife writes me love notes and puts them in my lunch box every Friday," says Daniel, father of a ten-year-old daughter. "She writes things like, 'I love you,' 'I miss you,' 'I can't wait to have some time with you.'"

"We sing in the choir together every Sunday," relates Brad, father of a two-year-old son.

"We rarely watch television in the evenings, whether or not the kids are with us," says Lori, the mother of three young sons. "No television helps teach our kids to entertain themselves so they aren't as demanding of our full attention, and my husband and I can talk."

"My husband and I try to take at least one walk alone each week," relates Diane, mother of triplet girls.

"When we have date nights, we always take turns surprising each other about the destination," reveals Claire, mother of two teen-age sons.

"We have been taking dance lessons once a week and love it!" says Marti, mother of a three-and-a-half-year-old son.

Whether you sing in the choir, take dance lessons or write love notes, creating your own rituals can make each of you feel loved and special. By creating these events, you are making a choice to love and to carry on your love for each other.

"Every night, the whole family sits down together and we have dinner by candlelight," says Tony, father of two teen-age daughters. "We run up quite a candle bill, unless we go out to eat, but to me, this ritual is a necessary part of the day. We all sit down. We discuss anything exciting or troubling that happened to us that day, and all the tension seems to melt away. Then, after dinner, our daughters go do their homework, and my wife and I have coffee together. Nobody has a completely happy life, or a completely healthy situation. But the way we do it, I can't see doing it any other way."

A FINAL WORD

The other day, I bought my older daughter a pair of roller skates. She had been asking me for skates, and I thought it would be fun for her to learn to roller skate. As I watched her trying to learn, I noticed that she fell down sometimes, but she always picked herself up, no complaints. After several days of practicing, she slowly but surely began to actually skate. When a neighbor complimented her and asked how she learned to skate so well, she replied: "Oh, whenever I fell down I just got back up."

Often, our own children can teach us a lot about life and love. In our own struggles as parents and lovers, we may fall down sometimes in our efforts to love, but we can get back up again.

It is not always easy to find the time to make love, or to muster the energy to love. There are times when we come home from a hard day at the office and perhaps wish we were walking into that quiet apartment we may have had when we were single. There are days when we have just reached the limit of our patience and capacity to be loving and just "lose it," and yell at the kids and our spouse. There are days when we wonder if there is any space left in the house for "our things," when every knook and cranny seems to be taken up with toys, clothes that are not our size, strollers or highchairs, baseball gloves or teen magazines. There are days when we would like to "chuck everything" and move to Tahiti! These are all normal feelings and you are not alone. *We have all been there.*

When we became parents, most of us made that choice. What we didn't realize and what no one told us, is how hard it is to raise children to be happy and healthy, and at the same time try to maintain a loving, sexually fulfilling relationship with our spouse. But just as you *chose* to have the children you adore, you can also *choose* not to allow all the difficulties entailed in raising children to erode the love you have for each other. You can make time for yourselves. You can make your bedroom a private place for just the two of you. You can teach your children to respect your privacy. You can find ways to be spontaneous lovers when opportunities present themselves or create opportunities. You can help each other to grab some self time to exercise or rest or pursue personal dreams or goals. You can keep telling yourselves that it is all right to be lovers and express your love in many pleasurable ways. And you can keep telling yourselves that it is perfectly all right to talk about your feelings and desires and dreams, and find ways to pursue and obtain your slice of personal happiness.

Being good lovers and good parents means that we do not live *for* our children but *with them.* By becoming martyrs and sacrificing everything for our children, we do them no favors. But when we consider our own happiness, too, and make the maintaining of our relationship a priority, we give our children a great gift—a sense of security and the capacity to grow into the happy, healthy adults we want them to be.

Love is hard and scary sometimes, but it can feel great, too! You may not ever be able to recapture exactly the same thrilling "high" you experienced when you first fell in love with each other, but you can come close to it when you give yourselves a chance to be lovers.

Hold onto your love. *Nurture it.* Then, when the day comes when you drop the kids off at college or when they leave home to make their own way in the world, you can glance at each other and smile— knowing, with just a look, that there is something special still going on. . .

ENDNOTES

INTRODUCTION
1. Sheila Kitzinger, *The Experience of Childbirth* (New York: Taplinger Publishing Company, Inc., 1972), 80.

CHAPTER 1: The Sex Hex: How We Lose Ourselves When the Kids Are Born
1. Carole Rafferty and Mark K. Powelson, "Love in the Nineties," *San Francisco Focus* (March 1988): 47.

CHAPTER 2: Sexpectations: How the Myths about Sex Appeal and Romance Keep Us from Having Both
1. Dr. Alan Loy McGinnis, *The Romance Factor* (San Francisco: Harper & Row, 1982), 18-19.
2. Lonnie Barbach, Ph.D., *For Each Other: Sharing Sexual Intimacy* (New York: New American Library, 1982, 1984), 219.
3. McGinnis, *The Romance Factor*, 8.
4. Barbara De Angelis, Ph.D., *How to Make Love All the Time: Secrets for Making Love Work* (New York: MacMillan Publishing, 1987), 134.

CHAPTER 3: Tunnel of Love or Tunnel Vision? Getting Your Priorities Straight
1. Paul Pearsall, Ph.D., *Super Marital Sex* (New York: Doubleday & Company, Inc., 1987), 9.
2. William H. Masters and Virginia E. Johnson in association with Robert J. Levin, *The Pleasure Bond: A New Look at Sexuality and Commitment* (Boston, Toronto: Little, Brown and Company, Inc., 1974), 260.
3. Ibid., 260.
4. Sanford J. Matthews, M.D. and Maryann Bucknum Brinley, *Through the Motherhood Maze, Survival Lessons for Loving Mothers... From an Outspoken Children's Doctor* (New York: Doubleday & Company, Inc., 1982), 8.
5. Pearsall, Ph.D., *Super Marital Sex*, 26.
6. Matthews, M.D. and Bucknum Brinley, Introduction to *Through the Motherhood Maze*.

CHAPTER 4: Connect and Conquer: How to Keep Parenting from Destroying Your Sexual Desire
1. Bill Cosby, *Fatherhood* (Garden City, New York: Doubleday & Company, Inc., 1986), 20.
2. Richard Ferber, M.D., *Solve Your Child's Sleep Problems* (New York: Simon and Schuster, 1985), 69-70.
3. Ibid., 77-78.
4. Edward F. Murphy, *2,715 One-Line Quotations for Speakers, Writers & Raconteurs* (New York: Crown Publishers, Inc., 1981), 81.
5. Ferber, M.D., *Solve Your Child's Sleep Problems*, 103.
6. David Gelman et al., "Not Tonight, Dear," *Newsweek* (October 26, 1987): 65.
7. Ibid., 66.
8. Dr. Benjamin Spock, *Experts Advise Parents: A Guide to Raising Loving, Responsible Children,* ed. Eileen Shiff, M.S., (New York: Delacorte Press, 1987), 228.
9. Marvin Silverman, Ed.D. and David A. Lustig, Ph.D., *Parent Survival Training: A Complete Guide to Modern Parenting* (North Hollywood, California: Wilshire Book Company, 1987), 99.

10. Lonnie Barbach, Ph.D., *For Each Other: Sharing Sexual Intimacy* (New York: New American Library, 1982), 252.

CHAPTER 5: Climax Interruptus: How to Cope with Interruptions in Flights of Fancy

1. Edward F. Murphy, *2,715 One-Line Quotations for Speakers, Writers & Raconteurs* (New York: Crown Publishers, Inc., 1981), 151.
2. Dr. Ruth K. Westheimer, "Discovering the Joys of 'Quickie' Sex," *Redbook* (July 1989): 113.

CHAPTER 6: Romance: How to Bring Out the Lover in Your Spouse

1. Paul Dickson, *Toasts: The Complete Book of the Best Toasts, Sentiments, Blessings, Curses, and Graces* (New York: Delacorte Press, 1981), 176.
2. Laurence Shames, "What Men Find Romantic (That Might Surprise You)," *McCall's* (February 1985): 16.
3. Edward F. Murphy, *2,715 One-Line Quotations for Speakers, Writers & Raconteurs* (New York: Crown Publishers, Inc., 1981), 15.
4. Carol Botwin, *Is There Sex After Marriage?* (Boston, Toronto: Little, Brown and Company, 1985), 104.
5. Jeanne M. Toal, "Why Tension Is a Turn-On," *Mademoiselle* (April 1988): 140.
6. Shames, "What Men Find Romantic," 14.
7. Kathleen McCoy, "5 Sex Secrets Women Wish Husbands Knew," *Reader's Digest* (January 1988): 94.
8. Nathaniel Brandon, Ph.D., "If You Could Hear What I Cannot Say: The Husband/Wife Communication Workshop," *Redbook* (April 1985): 94.
9. Gregory Stock, Ph.D., Introduction to *The Book Of Questions* (New York: Workman Publishing Company, Inc., 1985, 1987), 20, 22, 24, 29, 33, 41, 67, 91, 114, 152.
10. McCoy, "5 Sex Secrets," 93.

CHAPTER 7: Brief Encounters: Being Spontaneous When Spontaneity Seems Gone

1. William Betcher, M.D., Ph.D., *Intimate Play: Creating Romance in Everyday Life* (New York: Viking, 1987), 26.
2. Dr. Ayala M. Pines, *Keeping the Spark Alive: Preventing Burnout in Love and Marriage* (New York: St. Martin's Press, 1988), 171.
3. Dagmar O'Connor, *How to Make Love to the Same Person for the Rest of Your Life and Still Love It* (Garden City, New York: Doubleday & Company, 1985), 35.
4. Ibid., 35-36.
5. Anne Mayer, "Playing Together," *Bride's* (April/May 1983): 272.
6. Pines, *Keeping the Spark Alive*, 48-49.
7. Ibid., 171.

CHAPTER 8: "More Passion, Please!" How to Put the Fun Back into Your Sex Life

1. William H. Masters, Virginia E. Johnson and Robert C. Kolodny, *Masters and Johnson on Sex and Human Loving* (Boston, Toronto: Little, Brown and Company, 1985), 440-441.
2. Bernie Zilbergeld, Ph.D., *Male Sexuality: A Guide to Sexual Fulfillment* (Boston, Toronto: Little, Brown and Company, 1978), 19-20.
3. Lonnie Barbach, Ph.D., Personal communication with author, 1989.
4. Zilbergeld, *Male Sexuality*, 12.
5. Masters, Johnson and Kolodny, *Sex and Human Loving*, 5.
6. Kenneth Ray Stubbs, Ph.D., *Romantic Interludes: A Sensuous Lover's Guide* (Larkspur, California: Secret Garden, 1988), 11.

7. Masters, Johnson and Kolodny, *Sex and Human Loving,* 304.

8. Marty Klein, *Your Sexual Secrets, When to Keep Them, When and How to Tell* (New York: E.P. Dutton, 1988), 10.

9. William Betcher, M.D., Ph.D., *Intimate Play: Creating Romance in Everyday Life* (New York: Viking, 1987), 139.

10. Ibid., 148.

11. Sally Wendkos Olds, *The Eternal Garden: Seasons of Our Sexuality* (New York: Time Books, 1985), 22.

CHAPTER 9: For Better or for Worse? How to Look and Feel Good for Yourself and Your Spouse

1. Dr. Ruth K. Westheimer, "Oh, Grow Up!" *Redbook* (May 1987): 186.

2. Marilyn Elias, "Working Out Builds Women's Sex Drive," *USA TODAY* (November 11, 1988): D1.

3. Marilyn Elias, "Exercise Can Boost Sex Life of Folks over 40," *USA TODAY* (November 9, 1987): D1.

4. William H. Masters, Virginia E. Johnson and Robert C. Kolodny, *Masters and Johnson on Sex and Human Loving* (Boston, Toronto: Little, Brown and Company, 1985), 503.

5. Westheimer, "Oh, Grow Up!," 186.

6. A. G. Britton, "Thin Is Out, Fit Is In," *American Health* (July/August 1988): 60, 70.

7. Ibid., 71.

8. Richard B. Stuart and Barbara Jacobson, *Weight, Sex and Marriage: A Delicate Balance* (New York, London: W.W. Norton & Company, 1987), 34-35.

9. Ibid., 58.

10. Masters, Johnson and Kolodny, *Sex and Human Loving,* 453.

CHAPTER 10: Getting Away: How to Find Paradise in Hotel Heaven

1. Paula Scher, *The Honeymoon Book* (New York: M. Evans and Company, Inc., 1981), 185.

2. Paula M. Siegel, "Bugging Out: A Few Days Without the Kids Can Be the Best Thing *for* the Kids," *Parenting* (May 1987): 91.

CHAPTER 11: "I Need a Break!" How to Get Some "Self Time"

1. Henry David Thoreau, *A Week on the Concord and Merrimack Rivers, Walden, The Maine Woods and Cape Cod,* ed. Robert F. Sayre (New York: Literary Classics of the United States, Inc., 1985), 430.

2. Sharon Johnson, "Stealing Solitary Moments," *San Francisco Chronicle* (September 28, 1988): D3.

3. Vassilis Vassilikos, *The Plant, the Well, the Angel,* translated from Greek by Edmund and Mary Keeley (New York: Alfred A. Knopf, 1964), 131.

4. Meyer Friedman, M.D. and Ray H. Rosenman, M.D., *Type A Behavior and Your Heart* (New York: Alfred A. Knopf, 1974), 70.

5. Georgia Witkin-Lanoil, Ph.D., *The Male Stress Syndrome: How to Recognize and Live with It* (New York: Newmarket Press, 1986), 16.

6. Edward F. Murphy, *2,715 One-Line Quotations for Speakers, Writers & Raconteurs* (New York: Crown Publishers, Inc., 1981), 89.

7. Georgia Witkin-Lanoil, Ph.D., *The Female Stress Syndrome: How to Recognize and Live with It* (New York: Newmarket Press, 1984), 113-114.

CHAPTER 12: Partners in Love: Building a Lasting Relationship

1. Scott M. Peck, M.D., *The Road Less Traveled: A New Psychology of Love, Traditional Values and Spiritual Growth* (New York: Touchstone Book/Simon & Schuster, Inc., 1978), 133.
2. Dwight H. Small, *After You've Said I Do* (Westwood, New Jersey: Fleming H. Revel Company, 1968), 75.
3. Dr. Alan Loy McGinnis, *The Romance Factor* (San Francisco: Harper & Row, 1982), 197.

The Plant, the Well, the Angel, by Vassilis Vassilikos, translated from Greek by Edmund and Mary Keeley (Alfred A. Knopf, Inc., ©1964). Reprinted by permission. All rights reserved.

The Pleasure Bond: A New Look at Sexuality and Commitment, by William H. Masters and Virginia E. Johnson, with Robert J. Levin (Little Brown and Company, Inc., ©1974). Reprinted by permission of Masters & Johnson Institute. All rights reserved.

The Road Less Traveled: A New Psychology of Love, Traditional Values and Spiritual Growth, by Scott M. Peck, M.D. (Touchstone Books, published by Simon & Schuster, Inc., ©1978). Reprinted with permission. All rights reserved.

The Romance Factor, by Dr. Alan Loy McGinnis (Harper & Row Publishers, Inc., United States and Canadian rights only, ©1982). Reprinted with permission. All rights reserved.

Romantic Interludes: A Sensuous Lover's Guide, by Kenneth Ray Stubbs, Ph.D. (Secret Garden, ©1988). Reprinted with permission. All rights reserved.

Solve Your Child's Sleep Problems, by Richard Ferber, M.D. (Simon and Schuster, ©1985). Reprinted with permission. All rights reserved.

"Stealing Solitary Moments," by Sharon Johnson, from *San Francisco Chronicle,* September 1988 (The New York Times Company, ©1988). Excerpted sections reprinted by permission. All rights reserved.

"The Stepparenting Dilemma," by Benjamin Spock, M.D., and Mary Morgan, from *Experts Advise Parents: A Guide to Raising Loving, Responsible Children,* edited by Eileen Shiff, M.S. (Delacorte Press, ©1987). Excerpts reprinted by permission of Lescher and Lescher, LTD. All rights reserved.

Super Marital Sex, by Paul Pearsall, Ph.D. (Doubleday, a division of Bantam, Doubleday, Dell Publishing Group, Inc., ©1987). Reprinted with persmission. All rights reserved.

"Thin Is Out, Fit Is In," by A.G. Britton, from *American Health,* July/August 1988 (*American Health,* ©1988). Reprinted with permission. All rights reserved.

Through the Motherhood Maze: Survival Lessons for Loving Mothers...From an Outspoken Children's Doctor, by Sanford J. Matthews, M.D., with Maryann Bucknum Brinley (Doubleday, a division of Bantam, Doubleday, Dell Publishing Group, Inc., ©1982). Reprinted with permission. All rights reserved.

Toasts: The Complete Book of the Best Toasts, Sentiments, Blessings, Curses, and Graces, by Paul Dickson (Delacorte Press, ©1985). Reprinted by permission of The Helen Brann Agency, Inc. All rights reserved.

2,715 One-Line Quotations for Speakers, Writers & Raconteurs, edited by Edward F. Murphy (Crown Publishers, Inc., ©1981). Reprinted with permission. All rights reserved.

Type A Behavior and Your Heart, by Meyer Friedman, M.D. and Ray M. Rosenman, M.D. (Alfred A. Knopf, ©1974). Reprinted with permission. All rights reserved.